VOICES FROM THE BAYOU

VOICES FROM THE BAYOU

Baton Rouge Students Confront Racism, Police Brutality, and a Historic Flood

Baton Rouge Students

Foreword by Sister Helen Prejean

With an Introduction by Clarence Nero

Bayou Soul
Writers and Reader's Conference

Published in the United States by Bayou Soul Literary Conference

ISBN-13: 9781542932714
ISBN-10: 1542932718

Cover Design: Stuart Bache

Printed In The United States
10 9 8 7 6 5 4 3 2 1

First Edition

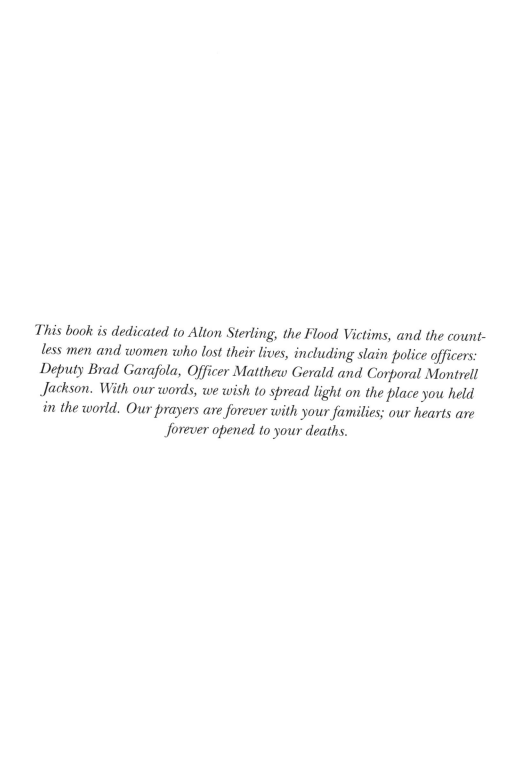

This book is dedicated to Alton Sterling, the Flood Victims, and the countless men and women who lost their lives, including slain police officers: Deputy Brad Garafola, Officer Matthew Gerald and Corporal Montrell Jackson. With our words, we wish to spread light on the place you held in the world. Our prayers are forever with your families; our hearts are forever opened to your deaths.

Now the war is not over, victory isn't won.
And we'll fight to the finish, then when it's all
done,
We'll cry glory, oh glory
We'll cry glory, oh glory
-John Legend and Common (Glory)

CONTENTS

FOREWORD

I was born and raised in Baton Rouge, Louisiana as a child of white privilege. My family was a kind and gentle bunch. We had help in the house, and for a long time they were my only access to African American culture; my understanding was very one-dimensional. It wasn't until I moved to the projects in New Orleans and began to learn from the people and my vision grew. Including my faith in Christ. Not the niceties of theology, but Christ in the flesh – of people suffering.

This volume of essays by students at Baton Rouge Community College is a brave journey into the windswept plains of honesty and clarity. Here, people of all ages and colors declare themselves and their identities in all their glorious ordinariness and truth; this step is the first toward the journey out of darkness and into the light of understanding. In it, these writers give themselves over to us as Other, so that we may see them for who they are, and in turn see ourselves a little more clearly for who we are. The result is a pioneering work of authentic voices from Baton Rouge, for Baton Rouge, and for the world.

Baton Rouge is less a small city and more a large town; often, this capital city dwells in the shadow of its much more famous sister city just 70 miles down the river. With the shooting of Alton Sterling and the police officers, and the flood of the summer of

2016 Baton Rouge became stamped in the cultural consciousness in the way that Ferguson, Missouri has come to signify cultural struggle. As I watched these tragedies unfold in my beloved hometown, what became clear to me was the pure calmness of the people of Baton Rouge. Unlike other American cities where the tragedy of violence by law enforcement has struck, Baton Rougeans of all colors remained peaceful and non-violent. The painful crack of gunfire on that quiet Sunday morning when Baton Rouge police officers were gunned down was perpetrated by someone who came to Baton Rouge from another place. Having for so long dwelled in the shadow of the Big Easy, a new identity of the Cow Town, the Big Raggedy, began to emerge that summer: Baton Rougeans became the gentle people, the people who didn't erupt into violence, riots, and hatred. This is the Baton Rouge that I know and love with all my life and heart.

The writers in this volume declare their identities as Baton Rougeans—honest, peaceful, hopeful, authentic people who want more than anything to accept and be accepted by the Other. I am proud and honored to join these real, beautiful voices and I invite you to join me.

Sister Helen Prejean
National Bestselling Author of *Dead Man Walking*

INTRODUCTION

I knew this wasn't going to be like any other semester. Due to historic flooding in the area, we were starting two weeks later than usual and, like many of the students in my English classes, I had spent the entire summer feeling anxious about events that had unfolded in the once quiet and laid-back town of Baton Rouge. It started with the police shooting of Alton Sterling in early July, and the tension never let up. Once quiet streets were now filled with protesters who had come from far and near to fight for justice in the Alton Sterling shooting. I was one of those protesters who had marched with a peaceful crowd from the city police station to the State Capitol. Although I had seen TV reports of many other instances of police shootings of black men in places like Baltimore and Ferguson, Missouri, I just never thought this type of drama would happen in Baton Rouge, which is about an hour from New Orleans. Most of the action in this region usually occurs in New Orleans: Mardi Gras, Jazz Fest—and senseless murders. Sure, we've had our issues with violence like any other city, but I can't recall anything that approaches the magnitude of what happened in the aftermath of the Alton Sterling case.

Then, less than two weeks later, when innocent Baton Rouge police officers were murdered by a black man who wasn't even from the area, I thought I was suddenly living in the twilight zone. My heart was broken, and I wondered what happened or was happening to my America. Of course, I knew the long and infamous history of racism in the country and the reports of police shootings of unarmed black men, but I had never seen it up close and personal—and neither had my students at Baton Rouge Community College. Then, the heavy rains came in early August, leaving much of the city and surrounding parishes under water. As tragic as the flood was, it brought us together as a community. I saw whites helping to rescue blacks and vice-versa. It wasn't about your skin color or neighborhood. All people saw was another human being in need. Our humanity was realized, and suddenly the events that had divided us across racial lines seemed foolish in light of the visible grief and hurt on the faces of people who had lost everything. It was devastating to see so many people displaced and suddenly homeless. I was one of the blessed ones spared from flooding on my street. Unfortunately, many of my students were some of the unlucky ones who didn't have a place to call home. They had been traumatized, and I honestly didn't know how we would get through the semester with any type of normalcy, given the gravity of the situation. But we did, bit by bit.

We started putting our lives back together and healing from the horrific events that had occurred over the summer the old-fashioned way: by talking and writing about it all. Knowing that I couldn't approach the semester in my usual manner, I decided to start with a movie called *Freedom Writers*. It was made from a book written by students in Erin Gruwell's high school English classes in Long Beach, California. Many of the students in her class were considered at risk. They bore stories inside of them filled with pain that many of us will never understand. Their lives had been marked by violence and extreme racism. Hatred was palpable on each of their faces. One way Ms. Gruwell was able to reach them, however, was through the power of the written word. She had her students read books about the Holocaust and challenged them to write their own narratives in journals: a process that became very transformative for them and Ms. Gruwell.

I decided to adopt a similar approach with my students after watching the film, but many of them were reluctant and even afraid to open up about their individual experiences with racism and the police. I can recall one of my white male students, Zachary, approaching me at the end of a class. He said after the Alton Sterling shooting, he'd had bad dreams of his black co-workers chasing him through a crowd of protestors and blaming him for the killing. He was scared to share his feelings about such sensitive issues as race. I encouraged him to do so, anyway.

Some of my students openly cried out in class just at the mention of the events from the past summer. It wasn't an easy process, but we worked through it. At the end of the assignment, many of the students said they felt uplifted to know that they were not alone in their feelings; that there were others going through the same pain and confusion. Above all, I found it to be such a profoundly healing experience for me and my students that I shared our classroom experiences with some of my colleagues at the college, and they, too, were struggling with ways to connect and thought narrative writing could possibly be the answer to their prayers. Ultimately, I asked my colleagues, my students, and members of the Creative Writing Club—where I was the advisor—to join me in a little exercise that involved writing and collecting narratives from our students around issues of race, policing, and the historic flood. We posted signs around the campus, announcing our intentions. This idea grew into a book that was driven by students in the Creative Writing Club.

As the Freedom Writers had done, these students expressed that they wanted to do something great and make a profound difference: to turn all the tragedies that happened in Baton Rouge into something positive. After reading each of their narratives, I knew that they had accomplished what they set out to do. I was beyond proud of them for having the courage to share their stories of growing up in southern Louisiana (and occasionally elsewhere in the South) and to talk about racism with such openness and honesty. The late Dr. Maya Angelou once said, "Courage is the most important of all the virtues, because without courage you can't practice any other virtue consistently."

In this book are collected the voices of students who witnessed firsthand the horror and ugliness of hatred during the killing of police officers and Alton Sterling as well as the beauty of humanity during the Great Flood of 2016, when blacks and whites put aside their differences to help one another. Through listening to their voices, we can't help but share in their struggles and be moved by the willingness of each writer to lay the burdens down on paper for all of us to witness. Their stories—told in their own voices—compose a fight for freedom like I have never seen before, and it was set in motion inside American classrooms, where the true leaders and thinkers are born.

Professor Clarence Nero and Author of *Cheekie: A Child out of the Desire*
Baton Rouge Community College

PART I

Racism

KELLY

LOVE IS LOVE

I was born and raised in a small country town in Livonia, Louisiana, where everybody knew everybody and everybody got along. I lived in an all-white neighborhood but went to school with children of other races. Growing up, I was a good child, and I was an honor student throughout my school years. I always had a lot of friends, black and white. I never saw color; we were friends, and their race wasn't an issue with me. Later on in my high school years, I had a crush on a football player who was black. We both were crushing on each other and would always flirt. We exchanged numbers and would talk and text, but only hung out during school hours. We began dating, but not everyone was in our business. People were judgmental and we didn't want to cause any drama. Yet, by the time I was in tenth grade, I was at a point where I didn't care about what people had to say or think about me dating outside of my race. Because of how I felt about my boyfriend, I let it be known that he and I were a couple. I never cared about people talking behind my back because I was going to do what I wanted to do, regardless. They made comments and there were rumors, but it just didn't bother me.

When my mom and dad heard that I was dating a black guy, they had different reactions. Some of her friends and family told my mother about my relationship, but she wasn't sure whether what she had heard was true. So, one weekend, there was a local town fair, and I asked her if I could go and she allowed me to. She drove me there and told me she would be back at a certain time to pick me up. I went on into the fair, knowing my boyfriend and I planned on meeting up there to spend time together. We were enjoying ourselves and hanging out near the video games when I turned around to see my mom standing there with this angry look on her face. She yelled, "Kelly Renea, what are you doing?" I replied, "I'm talking to my friend." She was furious. She then grabbed me by my wrist and told me we were leaving. She screamed the entire way on the ride home. She told me, "I let you go to the fair, and this is what the hell you do?" She used a lot of foul language along with the n-word the entire time she was fussing at me. She advised me not to ask her to go to any other function outside of school because I would not be going. She had trusted me and let me go, but I ruined that because she caught me with a black man. Well, my secret was no longer a secret. She now knew the rumors were true. My mom was totally against my relationship; she didn't approve of my choice at all. She was always screaming, "I didn't raise you like that!" On the other hand, my father didn't have a problem with my relationship. He was a cool, laid-back type of person. As long as I was happy, he was fine with it. I told my mom how I felt about the situation and told her I was going to continue dating my friend. My mom was so stuck on the beliefs of her father—and warned that if he found out, he would disown me as his grandchild. She wasn't having that! My grandmother had no private objection to what I chose to do, but because of my grandfather, she had to go along with him. My grandfather was a good man, but his racist ways were ignorant. The racism was passed along through his family. I never knew his side of the family, but what I did know was that they had no dealings with blacks and they were very racist. I don't know what happened to make them this way, but I didn't like it. I hardly would visit my grandparents, mainly because of how racist they were.

My mom and I continued to bicker about this situation. She would always say that she didn't raise me like this. I was so sick of hearing that. Every day, I would hear the same old thing, over and over, and it got on my nerves. I always argued the point with her because I wanted to know why my dating a guy of another race was such a disgrace to our family. I expressed my view that he was just like any other guy and that, regardless of his color, we all bleed the same. Nevertheless, she was so stuck in her own ways because of my grandfather and what she feared family and friends would say. In other words, my mom was racist to a certain extent, but only because of her father, a reason which was completely absurd.

As time passed, more and more white girls at school were dating black guys. People would stare and mumble under their breath about the other girls and me, but we didn't care. There was talk about girls sneaking out to meet their friends, cutting class, and all kinds of things, but I never went that far. My education came first. By my senior year of high school, the racial slurs and criticism were simply not a factor. I have always stood to never see color, to instead see what is in the heart. All I knew was that my black boyfriend who was a star football player was in my heart and I wasn't losing what we had together because of any petty racist comments anyone made.

Racism is a problem all over America, but why? No one male or female of any race is any better than the next. We are all equal! I will never, have never judged anyone because of race, and I will not ever condone racist ways. I have dated out of my race since I was a teenager, and in 2004 I married a black man and conceived one of three biracial children. I love my children and I teach them to treat everyone equally. I raise my children to respect and love everyone, regardless of race.

Over the last twenty years, I have thought less about race. It is possible to live in Louisiana as a white liberal and think little about it, to convince yourself that most of the crude past is behind you. I live in an integrated neighborhood where my kids have friends of all colors; where I live now is diverse compared to where I grew up. Outward signs suggested things were different from that era, but on July 5, 2016, a 37-year-old Alton Sterling, a black man, was shot several times by a Baton Rouge police office while being held to the ground by other officers. This sparked outrage in the city where I live. Sterling's death is the latest in a long string of police shootings in the US to lead to public outrage and condemnation, particularly from Black Lives Matter and other movements against racial disparities in the criminal justice system. To many critics, the killing of Alton Sterling is just another example of an issue that quickly rose to the national spotlight after the police shooting of Michael Brown Jr. in Ferguson, Missouri, in August 2014. Black people are much more likely to be killed by police than their white peers. That sounds ridiculous, but it is based on facts. Never in a million years would I have thought that something like this would ever happen where I reside.

Racism is alive and well throughout the South, especially here in Louisiana. I am originally from Louisiana, and most of my family live here. You can clearly see the racism in everyday life no matter where you go. This problem is not completely due to the whites either. Louisiana is racism at its worst. It is the "good ole boy" system every day. It is not over. This is so sad, but true. We are all God's children, so why should we be at war with one another because of differences? Let's all get together, assist each other, and succeed in life. We need to not let racism tear us apart. The diversity here can be a source of strength. The history is great; the food is terrific, but many people seem to think a little more melanin makes one race superior to another.

HAILEY
LOVE ME AS I AM

B efore I came out of the womb, I was already forced to fight in a war that I had no clue I was even involved in. No weapons, just a biracial target trying to make it out alive. Growing up in old Metairie right outside of New Orleans, I was in a crossfire. It was very rare to see black people in that area unless they were working in a grocery store. As far as living there at that time, twenty years ago, I don't think so. The white people on this side of town felt like they had the upper hand. They didn't feel like black people were important. My white grandparents were some of those people. They were stuck on their old mores and values, even when one day my mother decided she wanted to be with a black man and was pregnant for one. My grandparents didn't approve, put my mother out on the streets, and disowned her.

As a child at the time, I didn't understand anything, but as I got older, to hear that my grandparents wanted nothing to do with me because of my skin color was hurtful.

I was told that they didn't even want to take the time to get to know my father because he was a young black man. Although my father had a full-time job, kept a roof over our heads, clothes on our backs, and food on the table, and took care of my mother and me, my grandparents still hated him. But one unforgettable night changed everything.

While my grandparents were sleeping in the comfort of their home, someone broke into it and held them at gunpoint. The intruder told them they had five seconds to give up all of their personal belongings or else he would kill them. Ironically, my dad was coming home from work just then and was the one who noticed that my grandparents' side window was open. In his mind, my dad was wondering, "Why would their window be open that late at night?" So, he went to check it out. He realized what was going on and immediately took action. He tackled the burglar from behind and fought him until the gun was out of reach. My grandmother quickly called the police, and my grandfather grabbed the gun and shot the intruder in the foot. The police soon arrived and took the man away in handcuffs. All my grandparents could to at that point was thank my dad and apologize to him for all they had said about him. From that day forward, they didn't judge any man by the color of his skin. Finally, my family was at peace, and I didn't have to deal with the drama anymore.

As a biracial child, it scares me to see what's going on around me. Yes, my family is at peace, but not the rest of the world. Even today, in 2016, I still face my own battles being of mixed race. I won't say all people do, but a good handful judge me based on my skin color. Some white people look on me as if I am a "mutt," and the black people don't care too much for me because they believe I think I am better than everyone else. They feel like because I'm in the middle, I get everything handed to me. They feel everything in my little world is perfect when in reality that's not the case. I didn't get into certain organizations. I didn't get jobs because of the race I put on my application, and I don't get to date certain people of my color. A bunch of my friends call me "white girl" because of my hair texture. They tell me how I will never understand the struggles of a black woman because half of me is white. Where exactly do I fit in? That's a question I'm still trying to answer nineteen years later.

KAYLE

WAR ZONE

L ife has its own way of challenging you, and you have to seek solutions to overcome problems. If you think nothing very challenging could happen in the small town of Kentwood, Louisiana, you're wrong. Growing up in this rural town with a population of less than 2,500, I dealt with a diverse group of people: black, white, rich, and poor. The area is spread out, but it has two high schools, Jewel Sumner High and Kentwood High. The mixture of race and culture creates an environment that sometimes results in clashes. I attended Sumner High.

On a foggy Monday morning at school, I was in class when an argument broke out. I didn't know what the argument was about, but both students were sent to the office. Curious, I asked a classmate, "What were Nathan and Marcus arguing about?"

"They were about to fight because Nathan told Marcus that he was going to hang him," whispered Chasity.

"No talking!" shouted Coach Currier from across the room.

I turned around to face the front of the classroom, shaken that this had happened. Everyone knew that Nathan was racist. He pretended that he wasn't, but he always made comments that made you think otherwise.

By Tuesday evening at school, Nathan and his group of white friends started threatening and insulting more black male students. They were saying racial slurs such as "nigger" and threatening to hang and shoot the black males. The black girls grew tired of the mistreatment and fearful for the lives of the black males and decided to take a stand. We told the principal about what people were saying and about our concerns. He assured us that he would investigate; therefore, we thought something was going to be done. But nothing happened. That week, the group of white students continued threatening and insulting the black students. Since the Sumner High administration did not do anything, and we were fed up with the disrespect, the black students planned to declare "war" on the white students at lunch on Friday. Rumors about the fight spread throughout the school like wildfire.

Thursday, the day before the fight, school wasn't fun. Tension was visible on faces, for what started as an argument between two senior classmen had turned into a racial divide of the school. All everyone was doing was talking about the fight and what was going to happen. Freshmen and sophomores who didn't even know the guys wanted to fight. The black students had gotten together and planned how to dress and prepared for the fight. Some white students said they were our friends and were not against us, because they loved us. They said they were not racist and wouldn't disrespect us in any sort of way.

Finally, Friday arrived, and everyone was ready. At lunchtime, the black students stood on one side, the white kids on the other. Everyone was looking at the other side with hatred in their eyes. Students skipped class just to record the fight or to attend. Animosity filled the air. Nathan and the white students started throwing racial slurs, and Marcus and the other black students threw them back. In the middle of the argument, Nathan called the black students "a pack of niggers." At that, Marcus had had enough and threw the first punch. The war had begun. The entire yard of students began fighting, boys versus boys, girls versus girls, even girls fighting boys. Even the white students who had said they weren't going to fight the black students did so in the end. The fight was so bad, the police were called. They came dressed in riot gear, with dogs.

After the war had been fought, fifty to sixty students were expelled or suspended. There were numerous injuries: broken arms, broken jaws, busted lips. A lot of hair had been pulled out. The causalities could all have been avoided if the administration had spoken up, if people were not taught to hate someone because of the color of his or her skin, and if someone took the time to see things from someone else's point of view. The country and the world would be better off without racism. That people should be judged "by the content of their character," not by the color of their skin, is something that Martin Luther King Jr. said. In the end, we are all made up of flesh and bones. We all have a choice to help or to hurt one another.

BEING EQUAL TO ONE ANOTHER

Have you ever been picked on because of the color of your skin? In many places, this happens and is becoming more and more common, even though segregation was made illegal many years ago. The worst case of racial bias that I ever witnessed happened when I was in middle school. I observed some black kids picking on white kids because they thought the whites weren't equal. Some of those white kids looked dirty and poor, so people would pick on them for their lack of style. Sometimes the white kids would get beat up.

After seeing this for a while, I asked one of the white boys, "Why aren't you defending yourself?" His response was that it isn't easy being one of the only white kids in a public school system. To make him feel better, I started hanging out with him and found he was a cool guy. He was not concerned or bothered about being picked on and bullied. We played basketball, ate lunch, and even helped each other with homework. Some of my black friends would look at us and ask me why I was hanging with the kid. I would tell them, "Just because he is white does not mean that he is not a great guy to be around." Still, they would ridicule him and tell me that they wouldn't hang around him because he was an outcast and dirty. But because I was raised to love everyone in spite of their differences, I would just shake my head and walk away.

One day, the white boy told me that in physical education class, one of the other boys tried to take the ball away from him. I asked him why the black kid tried to take the ball from him. He answered by saying that the boy told him that he didn't want a white boy playing with the basketball. On hearing that, I became hurt and irate because some of the kids kept picking on him and treating him like he was dirt. During school, when he showed me the guy who did took the ball from him, I discovered it was one of my closest friends. I was in awe and sad because I never thought that one of my best friends would be a bully. I told that friend that I do not hang with bullies and suggested he apologize. If not, we would not be friends anymore. He expressed to me that as long as I hung with the white kid, he did not want to be my friend anyway. The very same day, the white boy told me that he never thought being white in a predominantly black school would be this hard and that he wished that there were more kids like me.

Afterwards, I got to thinking about what he said. I figured if I could treat him as an equal, maybe I could get others to act the same way. The next day at school, I told everybody to stop looking at him as a white kid, to look past that and see the kindness in him. Some people followed my advice, while some of them still had hatred in their hearts. Sometimes he would cry and even miss school because of bullying, but I would call him and tell him, "Man, it's going to be all right." One day, we had to dress up in our best attire and he came with some beat-up shoes on; his idea of dressing up was to wear some pants that were too short and a dingy white shirt. The bullies laughed at him and stepped on his shoes. When I saw this, I immediately asked him if he was all right and told him that I would call my mom to bring him some of my clothes and shoes.

When people saw him with those clothes and shoes on, they tried to figure out how he could afford them and when he had changed into his outfit. He told them that I had given him the items, which amazed them. They even asked me why I let that boy wear my stuff. I told them it was because he was my friend.

Before we got out for the holiday break, I was so fed up with the bullying and racial tension towards him that I made a New Year's resolution. It was to encourage everybody to stop picking on him. So I started asking people, "What would you do if one of your brothers or sisters was coming home daily saying that they were getting picked on?" Most of them thought about it and said that I was right because they would want to fight. The day we got back from the holiday break, I saw almost the whole school speaking to my white friend and greeting him with kindness. I even saw people playing basketball with him and giving him Christmas cookies. That was one of the happiest moments of my life because when he first came to the school, he was targeted and bullied. But after I talked to people, they finally came around. They realized that he wasn't such a bad guy to hang around with after all. I also stopped seeing people curse at him and heard them actually calling him by his name. He was so happy that he even started to come to school with a smile on his face rather than fear in his eyes. He told me, "Tabias, I don't know what happened at first that caused everybody to hate me. One thing I do know is that I feel better now that everybody is my friend, and I hope it stays like this."

The next semester, I found out that he was transferring to another school. That had me sad because I thought, Right, just when everybody had started to get use to him, he has to transfer. But then a smile would come on my face when I went down the hallway and everyone asked me where he was. They hoped he would come to school. When I told them he was transferring, everybody was sad because he was such a cool dude with lots of potential. Even the guys and girls who had been bashing him every day missed him.

When he came back to school to get transfer papers, people were giving him so much love and asking why was he leaving. When I saw that, I almost busted out in tears because I knew it was my talking to everyone that made this change happen. As soon as he saw me, he said, "Thank you, Tabias, for being a friend."

In conclusion, I simply want people of this world to treat others like they want to be treated. I am tired of seeing the racial tension persist when the white and black relationship is what Martin Luther King Jr. was fighting for in the '60s. I just want everyone to know that just because they are white, black, or another race, that does not mean that they are better than the next person.

RAISING A POTENTIAL HASHTAG

B ecoming a mother was not always a dream of mine. With all the things I had endured as a child, I swore off being a mother. I had learned the saying, "The way your parents raised you is an indication of how you're going to raise yours someday," and I couldn't let that come to pass. I didn't have the happiest childhood, and I couldn't imagine re-creating that same nightmare for my own child. Imagine growing up in a household where you were deprived. You may be thinking of all the obvious things a child might be denied, but my experiences were not typical. My siblings and I weren't denied a two-parent household. We certainly were not deprived of food, shelter, or clothing. What we lacked was something much deeper. We lacked emotional attachment and mental stability.

We grew up in a household with constant arguing, belittling, name calling, resentment, and mistrust. The total lack of communication and expressions of love made us feel that we didn't have a voice. The anger my father and stepmom felt for one another was dispersed onto the children. As a child, I can remember being thrown through a wall—not against the wall, but through it. I was choked, slapped, whipped with an extension card, gym belts, switches, brushes, and any other creative items my parents could access. For one form of punishment, we had to kneel on raw rice until our knees bled. Sometimes, we had to do rigorous exercises until our muscles ached, and we cried out in agony.

It would be wrong of me to mention all the nightmares without also mentioning that there were good times along the way as well. We enjoyed family trips together, dining out, visits to the movie theater, skating rink outings, and times spent together laughing over a funny incident that occurred. Although there were good times, the walls of our home held so much hurt and pain that the good times were always outweighed by the bad. The occasional smiles and laughs here and there seemed to be a temporary fix to cover the open wounds that the bad times caused. We always knew that happy times would be overtaken by the anger. With each encounter, I knew that I would never pass this anger on to a child.

As a teenager, I didn't know much about love or what the proper way of raising a child was, and in a way, I don't think my parents did either. Parenting doesn't come with a manual. My difficult childhood may have been influenced by the way my parents were raised. The lessons that were taught to them, the experiences they had, the manner in which they were spoken to, disciplined, and punished, may give insight as well into why they raised my siblings and me in the manner they did. Also, the trauma from past relationships and the cruelty this world spews out may be other factors. Our parents do not always disclose to us all that they endured that shaped their thinking and actions. I often wonder about the experiences of my parents that formed them into providers but not nurturers. Their complicated methods prevented them from providing me with all that I needed to be "whole" as a child and later an adult. The lack of emotional attachment and mental stability, coupled with the abuse, created dysfunction, insecurities, and substantial amounts of hurt not only for the children but also for my parents. These were the very reasons I ran away from home far too soon.

I was still in high school and didn't know how to properly take care of myself, but I was willing to take that chance to experience an ounce of happiness. I went into the world looking for the missing components my parents had failed to give me and hoping that strangers could fill the void my parents had created over the years. I was literally "looking for love in all the wrong places." Due to this, I found myself in several situations where all traces of my morals and values had diminished. All that was left was this empty shell of a girl I could no longer recognize. I was filled with hurt and bitterness, and a sense of being lost. Things that I never could imagine happening began to unfold, and my life began to quickly spiral out of control. I developed a drinking problem and started smoking marijuana to escape my challenges and the reflection of the unknown girl I had become. I lost pieces of myself when I was molested by my cousin's husband, one of the many people I went to live with after leaving home. I was also raped twice by two men I barely even knew. I felt shame after each incident, and the little innocence that was left dwindled. Generally, after a woman is raped or molested, two things either occur: either they shy away from sexual encounters and associate sex with the trauma, or they become promiscuous as a way to gain back the control they felt they lost. The latter occurred with me. I used sex as a weapon. I used it to control whomever I was dating or to seduce men. I found myself in several empty relationships and even an abusive one.

Life was very hard for a while as I tried to refigure out who I was and what I wanted. It seemed like no matter how hard I tried to stay out of trouble, it found me and enticed me. I know now that the reason behind this was the lifestyle I lived and the company kept. At twenty-two, I was exhausted mentally and drained emotionally. After three years of turbulent independence, I finally broke down and moved back to Baton Rouge, or as we refer to it, the Big Raggedy. I desperately needed stability and a fresh start.

If you had told me back then that I would finally get my life together four years later and that I'd meet a man who would show me how to love and value myself, I probably would not have believed you. This strong, intelligent, hardworking black man came into my life and didn't try to change me, but instead showed me the love that I was desperately seeking. The changes in me that followed after I met him were voluntary. After being with him for a few years, I began to yearn for a child. I realized I could put my childhood behind me and be the parent I desired and not the type my parents were to me. The road to becoming a mother was not an easy one. I almost lost my life in my third trimester, but when has anything ever been easy for me? I fought through and by the grace of God I was blessed with a beautiful baby boy.

I knew that raising a black boy into manhood was not going to be an easy task. I'm always reminded of this every time a black boy or man is shot down in cold blood by police officers, who have taken God's appointed job into their hands. Black men and women have never been viewed as intellectual equals of whites in America, land of the supposedly free and home of the cowardly. How do I explain to my son that as a baby/toddler, he is cute and friendly, but as he ages, he will be seen as a threat to society? How do I explain to him that no matter how properly he speaks, no matter the number of degrees he attains, he will still be seen as a potential thief, thug, murderer, conniving, two-bit hustler, and target practice for racist police officers who don't view blacks as being deserving of life? It is up to me to show my son love, what love looks like, and how to love. It is up to me to instill in him that he is a strong, intelligent, handsome individual, and he's deserving of love, respect, equality, and opportunity. It is up to me to teach him how to value himself. Every morning before he goes to school, I will make it my priority to play James Brown's song "Say It Loud—I'm Black and I'm Proud." I can hear myself singing, "Say it loud," and his response will be "I'm black and I'm proud."

When I look at my son, I am afraid. I am afraid because I don't know how to explain to him that he will never be good enough in some white people's sight. I am afraid because he is going to start experiencing racism in elementary school from teachers who are afraid to teach a black boy out of fear of his rising and being better than their expectations of him. I have often wondered if it would have been better if I'd had a daughter, but then I'm reminded of Sandra Bland and countless other black women who have been slain, and I realize no matter the gender of my child, he or she will still face the same dilemma because of the melanin in their skin. Raising my son in America won't be an easy task, but when has anything in my life ever been uncomplicated?

DARNESHA
NO MORE DRAMA

L ooking back on life and my high school days, I was in lust with a guy three years older than me. Reality hit when at sixteen and in the eleventh grade, I was pregnant. While my mother had always spoken highly of me, she could no longer look at me. Knowing her baby girl was pregnant with no financial income was heartbreaking for her. I always saw myself being with my daughter's father, but it all went sour. Not even seven months into the pregnancy, he started being physically and verbally abusive. The abuse was on and off, just as our relationship was on and off. As time went on, the abuse got worse, but we eventually moved in together. My daughter saw me graduate high school, and shortly after high school, I started working at a department store in Zachary, Louisiana. Occasionally, my child's father came into the store, causing scenes and bringing home arguments into my work area.

One day he came into my work environment while I was checking out customers. He walked behind the register, pulled on my arm, and was about to hit me in the face when two male coworkers stopped him and escorted him out the building. Feeling humiliated and hurt, I realized I had to leave to save myself from being in a critical condition. I walked away from the register to catch my breath and saw a customer's son, who was white, bring me a note from his mother. I opened the note and saw that she had given me a hundred-dollar bill. Her note said, "I'm sorry for what you're going through, just let go and let God handle the rest."

Being in the heart of Zachary, you never know what you're going to get from a different race. Some white customers wouldn't speak when spoken to by a black person; others would lay their money on the counter while my hand was held out for the money. However, this woman didn't see color; she saw another human being who was hurt and needed help. That gave me a new perspective: that all white people aren't racist. I saw the customer giving me the letter as God speaking through her to get to me. I knew I couldn't ignore the fact that it was time that I moved on and got the drama out of my life that my child's father was causing me. Even though I knew in my mind I had to leave, I just wanted my daughter to always be under the same roof as her father. When I was growing up, my father wasn't around; I didn't want my daughter to grow up trying to fill a void the way I had. But many days, she wiped tears away from my eyes. The longer I stayed and put up with the abuse, I realized my daughter wasn't happy. She had started showing signs of unhappiness, by not talking much and not being the playful child I was used to seeing. Later that night after the woman gave me the note and money, I told myself this was not what I wanted. My daughter wasn't happy witnessing all the toxic things around her, and most of all I wasn't happy.

Hearing that I was going to leave made my daughter's father furious. He slapped me so hard I saw stars. He dragged me to another room in our apartment by my hair. After that, he told me I wasn't going anywhere, and locking the top lock on our front door, he left. I didn't have a key to unlock that top bolt, so my daughter and I were stuck inside the apartment. Being locked inside there, I couldn't do anything but think. I thought about how the ongoing situations were affecting my child and how lost I felt. I started pleading to God, asking for a way out and praying for a better life-style. When he came back, I pretended to be asleep. Then, when he went in the bathroom, I ran. He realized I left and ran after me, but he didn't catch me and went back for our daughter. While running in the rain to the local gas station, I felt hopeless, only because I had left my daughter in his toxic presence. I called my sister to pick me up, and the next day my family and I went to get my daughter and our belongings. I felt a huge weight being lifted off my shoulders.

Here I am today sharing something so traumatizing. I had never thought I'd be in that trapped situation. It made me stronger and wiser, because now I know not to trust so easily. My release came because of the one kindhearted white customer who gave me the push to walk by faith.

KETURAH

BOOT CAMP LOVE

igh school isn't as bad as most people portray it to be. I, personally, didn't finish high school, but the years I did attend were grand. I had many friends and favorable teachers. During my tenth-grade year, though, I was expelled from school. My mother decided to put me in a program called Louisiana National Guard Youth Challenge Program, or YCP for short. There I would attain my GED in place of my high school diploma. YCP is a military boot camp–based program. I'd exercise every day, and I'd have to abide by certain rules and regulations. At YCP I made a lot of friends and achieved my goal to graduate. The worst part about boot camp was having D squad: a correctional action the authorities there use to punish the students who have misbehaved. Basically, the one punished must exercise for twelve hours straight: no break, no excuses. I only got into trouble one time at YCP, and I'll never forget why.

One day in YCP, my friend Luttrell and I were lying down in our room during rest time, just talking. Our other two roommates, Wilbert and Madison, had just left to go to the bathroom. Three minutes passed by and suddenly Madison came running back into our room like a madwoman. Her eyes were red, and her face was screwed up like she wanted to cry. She kept saying, "Oh my God!" I asked her what was wrong, and she said, "Wilbert just called you and Luttrell 'niggers'!" When Madison told us what Wilbert said, Luttrell's face dropped. I was shocked as well. I had never been called a "nigger" by someone of another race before. I didn't know how to feel, so I asked Madison to tell us all that Wilbert said. Madison replied, "When me and Wilbert left, she said, 'Ugh, I can't stand them two.' I asked, 'Who? Keturah and Luttrell?' She said, 'Yes. They're always laughing and snickering, but I guess the niggers can't fight their natural instincts, coming from the hyenas and all.' " I walked away to cool off after hearing this account. "Can you believe that, Keturah?" Madison asked me. I replied with a simple "no." In my head, I was still perplexed, but I couldn't fight the feeling of anger beginning to build inside me. I began to remember the time I was in elementary school and we spoke about racism during Black History Month. I remembered how badly black people were treated during the early, middle, and late 1900s. I hadn't thought racism still existed, but it was perfectly clear to me that it absolutely did exist.

When I finally snapped back to reality, I grabbed Luttrell's wrist and got up. Madison asked, "What are y'all about to go do?"

I said, "I'm about to go confront her." Madison followed us.

As Luttrell and I walked out of our room, Wilbert was leaving the bathroom. When she and I made eye contact, I instantly became enraged. I began to walk faster towards her. The look on her face assured me that she was aware of the reason Luttrell and I were approaching her. Wilbert stopped walking midway down the hall. When I got close enough to her, I said, "Would you like to repeat to me and Luttrell what you stated to Madison?" There was complete silence at that point. Madison looked as if she didn't want to be affiliated with the situation. Luttrell looked like she was ready to fight. I took a long deep breath and repeated, "Would you like to repeat to me and Luttrell what you stated to Madison?!"

Wilbert looked at both Luttrell and me, then back at me, and just smiled. She said, pointing to Madison, "If I wanted to call you a 'nigger,' I'll say it to you and not her. You people are always ready to fight and cause hell. How about you just go back from where you came?"

Luttrell responded, "'You people'? And who is 'you people'?"

"You people . . . You *black* people. You know, Negro," Wilbert said while laughing.

Madison's face turned red listening to Wilbert's insults towards Luttrell and me. "So, you didn't call Luttrell and Keturah 'niggers' as we walked to the bathroom?" Madison interrupted.

"Oh, I never said I didn't," Wilbert stated. "I said if I wanted to call them 'niggers,' I would've told them and not you, that's all."

Every time I heard Wilbert say that word, it was like someone was splashing me in the face with boiling hot water. It made me furious to see that she really had the audacity to laugh in our faces and be completely obnoxious, cocky, and rude enough to call African Americans "niggers." I was fed up, and tired of hearing Wilbert's disrespect for me and my race. After just standing there glaring at her for a while, I slapped Wilbert in the chest two quick times and said, "You don't have to admit to calling us 'niggers' in our face, but know this: If you ever call me that word directly, I'll beat all the pretty little white off your ugly ass. Got it? Oh, and I'm going to address the fact that you're a racist to the Cadres, and tell them that I don't feel comfortable with having a racist in the same room as me."

Luttrell laughed and said, "Yeah, and she has one, two, three witnesses."

Wilbert's face immediately turned red hot like apple candy. "Don't ever touch me again, Keturah, and as far as you beating my ass, we'll see," she rebutted. Then she turned around and walked off, shouting, "I can't wait! I don't want to be in a room with wild monkeys anyway." My heart sank and my mouth dropped.

The other girls came to their doors to see who it was that had spewed such a horrible insult. I remember thinking to myself, Is this girl insane? Before I knew it, I was running down the hallway after her. I grabbed a handful of Wilbert's hair from behind and threw her to the floor. Wilbert yelled, "I thought I told you not to ever touch me again you, stupid filthy nigger!" Without thinking twice, I hopped on top of her and elbowed her in the mouth twice. I then got up and grabbed her hair and proceeded to smash her face repeatedly against the railing on the side of the wall until the Cadres came to break the fight up. My main goal at that time was to knock all her teeth out of her mouth so that she could never call anyone else a 'nigger.' I successfully knocked out three, and that was satisfactory for me.

My reaction in this racist situation ended in violence. That wasn't the right way, but having to deal with racial slurs is not fair. I was raised to love everyone equally. It's not about whether you're black or white, blue orange or green; it's about what is in your heart and the type of person you are inside if I choose to dislike you. I was taught about segregation and informed that everyone doesn't like everybody. Even though I wasn't born during the time that racism was prevalent and out in the open in America, I have experienced it. I can honestly say being called a 'nigger' that day didn't feel good at all. In fact, it was the worst feeling I had ever felt in my life. I felt so low, like I didn't belong. I felt abandoned and alone. Wilbert really made me feel like she was better than me, but she wasn't. We all bleed red blood, have the same organs needed to survive and function inside our bodies. We all need to eat and sleep. Racism isn't a foreign subject, but it is an ideology that is destroying the world and needs to end.

ROBERT
OPPRESSION ON THE JOB

In the year 2015, I worked at a plant with a lot of different races. I was put on the carpenter crew, and the majority of my crew was Caucasian. I was the only African American, and there was one Hispanic guy. It seemed like I was the one whom the majority felt the need to make jokes about. Every morning, after we clocked in, we would head to our print shack where we had morning meetings. They would say things like, "What you brought for lunch today? Fried chicken and grape juice?" And they would laugh. I knew exactly what they were getting at. I paid no mind to it because I knew what the consequences would be if I entertained them.

One day the boss split the crew in half to complete two projects. I wasn't feeling well, and the heat wasn't making it better. One of the guys felt like he wanted to clown and make jokes, saying, "Come on, Rob, pick up the work before I crack the whip on your ass." It pissed me off, so I grunted and bit my tongue to keep from telling him what was really on my mind. I continued working but with a pissed-off attitude. He made one more joke, not realizing it was going to be the last. The comments got under my skin and I retaliated, exactly what they were expecting out of me. I told him, "I'm sick of putting up with the racist jokes you guys been making."

"Nigger please!" he said. I dropped my tools and threw a punch at him. He got exactly what he wanted: me off the crew and fired.

I regret that day and I wish I would have handled things differently. I could have ignored him or gone and told a higher authority. It sparks so much anger in me to know that African Americans are still getting picked on like this. Many, but not all, Caucasians say and do cruel things to push us to our limit. Slavery ended over a hundred fifty years ago, yet times have not changed as far as white and black segregation. It's time for a change.

African Americans have struggled for many years trying to gain equality. Unfortunately, inequality and racism are some of the main issues in America today. I have experienced racism first-hand and the anger that it sparks inside.

ZAIN

MY DREAM OF AMERICA

Many people who live outside the United States think it is the most beautiful country in the world. People in developing countries, like my mother's home country, Pakistan, idealize America as a place where life changes. They view the US as a modern-day version of Thomas More's *Utopia*, where you step outside the airport and an expensive Mercedes is waiting for you, with beautiful women who have fancy fans. Indeed, it was difficult to digest that America, after all, does not resemble the Utopian view. Once, an American resident who came to Pakistan informed me that "America has freedom of who you want to be and what are your views." However, I did not see that when I landed in America. We came to a very small city in the state of Tennessee and, sadly, there was no Mercedes or expensive car waiting outside for us. Yet I was hopeful and still content to be in America.

The next day was my first day of high school. I was very excited to go to a high school in America. I previously had seen in a few Hollywood movies that high schools have a very friendly environment, but my knowledge was all just a myth. At the school I went to in the small town of Jackson, 90 percent of the students were African American, and I was the only one of my race and nationality. Before going to the school, I wondered how I would be able to make friends there, where no one resembled me in color or nationality. However, a hope was still brewing due to my exposure to Hollywood on TV. I was confident that the United States was far from the era of racism and discrimination.

My first school experience did not agree with my predictions. When I entered the school, I noticed that students were looking at me with weird stares. I thought it was because I was new in school and that everybody was simply curious about me. However, while I was walking towards my first class, I heard somebody whispering that "We have a terrorist in the school." I initially ignored such comments because I did not realize that they were directed towards me. When I entered my first class, the teacher asked us to stand up, one student at a time, and introduce ourselves to everyone. Upon my turn, as soon as I spoke, my peers began to laugh at me, and I didn't understand the reason behind their giggles. I asked myself, Am I saying something wrong? There was a possibility that their reaction was caused by the way I sounded. I was a little embarrassed, so I just pronounced my name and quickly sat down. After the introductions, a group of kids approached my desk. They referred to me as "a terrorist." Those words, I will never forget in my life. I wandered around in my mind to find a possible reason for being called a terrorist: Had I harmed them? Had I done something to induce terror or fear amongst them? Or is it that my very existence, color, race, and nationality automatically assign me the tag of terrorist? This was just the first day of school, and I did not even speak to anyone in the class or make any efforts towards making new friends. Some students gathered around me and started to ask me some astonishing questions: "Where the bombs at? Hey, do you know Osama bin Laden? Was he your uncle or was he your father? Are you going to bomb this school?" With the limits of my temper and emotionality being crossed, tears started appearing in my eyes. I was only fifteen. How can one think a fifteen-year-old could even devise such a plan? A fifteen-year-old-boy who is innocent and emotional, who had traveled across the world, was being blamed for something that he was completely oblivious to. Consequently, I told the teacher I had to go home because I was sick. A school bus dropped me off at home with the permission of my parents.

Upon arriving home, I informed my mother of all the questions and astonishing interactions I encountered during my first day of school. Like a young adolescent who lost his toy, I hugged my mother's chest and cried a river of tears. After that day, I did not go to school for at least a week. Fear and anxiety kept me hesitant to face more encounters. I had never been bullied before, and I concluded that I had arrived at a rather dangerous place. I could not forget the questions my classmates had asked me. Those questions haunted me every day.

HOPE FOR TOLERANCE

On September 18, 2004, I met my best friend in the school bathroom, of all places. His name is Robert Oliver Newman Jr. Although Oliver is white, he is still my best friend to this day. We attended multiple schools together. We are both Catholic and even attend the same church.

A few years ago, Oliver and I went to his cousins' wedding rehearsal. I was having a good time with my friend when we noticed a white woman staring at me with disgust on her face. Under her breath, she quietly called me "black trash." How can someone feel hatred for a child? Oliver got mad at her and immediately flashed at her. I wasn't surprised at this woman's behavior because I knew racism was still alive and well in America. Generational hatred is killing our nation.

Racism comes in all shapes and forms. When I was younger, I was high-strung at school and would be put in TOR (time out room) basically every day in elementary school. Now, when I look back, I realize the TOR was my primary classroom and Mrs. Cole was my homeroom teacher. Taking a child out of the classroom in his early years prevents his access to building blocks that are vital to his future learning abilities. This disciplinary tactic causes many of our black children to fail.

Additionally, I stopped standing for the national anthem when I was in the eleventh grade at Redemptorist High School in Baton Rouge. The other kids genuinely didn't care what I was doing because we were a family or, as we put it, a "Wolfpack." I didn't want to stand and salute a flag for a country that supports racism and hatred, and other students supported me. Colin Kaepernick, a professional football player, has been in the news lately for protesting what he deems wrongdoings against African Americans and minorities in the United States. He doesn't stand for the national anthem either.

The thing about race is sometimes I feel like I'm in the middle. On one hand, I don't like the white race for what they did to us during slavery. They separated us by color, and today we do the same. You know the old adage "Divide and conquer." Sadly, the black race are still living with our ancestors' mentality. Also, many white folks continue to feel they are superior, as if it is their God-given right to believe they are better than everyone else. They are taught this by their parents. Look back through history; the white man has to put his touch on everything from the Bible to the naming of countries. But on the other hand, I'd like to look past all that and just see the good in everyone.

It's hard to look past skin color, though, when racism persists in America. When Barack Obama became president, for example, the media disclosed both the bad and good things he did. His birthright as an American citizen was put in question. I saw this as whites showing they didn't want a black man to lead the nation. They didn't think a person of color should be in such a high and esteemed position as the president. Furthermore, racism has been in existence since biblical time. During slavery, whites used the Bible, which by the way is written by the white man to enslave colored people. Napoleon also used the Bible to deceive colored people. Look at Egypt and Israel now. What color are the people?

Racism is alive in this country, and in other parts of the world, for many reasons:

- History – Because this is the way it has always been, this is the way we should do things now.
- Media – We notice more whites in commercials and on billboards, subtly suggesting white is right. We view movies that portray blacks in a negative limelight. We watch the nightly news reports of violent black acts.
- Denial – If we say it isn't so, then it isn't.
- Economics – Let's hire those who look like us.
- Human nature – We need to feel superior over someone else.
- Fear – Anything that is different to us is treated as a mark of danger and threat.

I believe racism can stop; I know it can. If everyone would just see each other as fellow human beings, brothers and sisters, the world would be a much better place. However, even though, as people, we understand the need to get rid of prejudices and treat everyone as equal and competent fellow-beings, will we? How we fix racism is a plight that has been going on for centuries, and will continue to do so, because to put it simply, human nature breeds disparity. As for me, to have a chance to survive the system, my mom says I need to be better than white folks. She says whites can be mediocre, but blacks need to be exceptional.

RACISM BEFORE OUR EYES

I can still smell the fresh finger paintings hanging in the sun to dry. I can still hear the roar of laughter coming from under the monkey bars. I can still see and will never forget the huge tears streaming down the chocolate face of my best friend on the playground. During my years in elementary school, I learned a lot about the big world around me, including the hurt that racial discrimination causes.

Being from the small community of Maurepas, nestled in the swamps of Louisiana, I had never seen or interacted with a person of color until I reached elementary school. During the first week of school, I met Kendra and Tyrone. They were twin African Americans who were in the same kindergarten class as me. I distinctly remember being amazed at the differences between my hair and skin and theirs. Their hair was more curly than mine and had a distinct, coarse texture.

Besides the obvious physical differences, the twins and I had major differences in our home lives and culture. The twins would make remarks about their father. Sometimes they would say that he liked whiskey a lot, or that he got home really late and wasn't very nice to them. Often times, Kendra would come to school with large bruises and scrapes. She always claimed that they came from the playground. Looking back, I'm sure there was more to the story. Tyrone would also have similar marks on his legs and would blame it on various things. As a child, I didn't put two and two together, but it is obvious to me now that the twins were abused.

By the time the twins and I reached fourth grade, we had become very close. Tyrone and I were closer due to our similar interests, such as basketball and baseball. One hot summer day after baseball practice, Tyrone invited me to his house. I did not ask my parents for permission, afraid they would tell me no. My parents were skeptical of Tyrone's family and were not fond of the black community on the outside of our small town. As I approached Tyrone's house, it seemed that his family felt the same about me as mine did about his. I didn't feel welcome, and it seems obvious now that there was racial tension. As a young boy, I did not understand why the twins' and my friendship was forbidden.

The next year was our final year in elementary school. We were finally fifth-graders, the big dogs of the school. We participated in the DARE program, went on the exciting fifth-grade field trip to the Audubon Zoo in New Orleans, and most importantly, found out who our friends really were. Our innocent minds were being influenced by outside opinions, the news, and other media that put thoughts into our heads. Kendra and Tyrone were still two of the few black students in the whole school. To my knowledge, they never faced bullying or discrimination because of their skin color until the end of our fifth grade year. At our very small school, we all considered each other friends and got along until one chilly day on the playground behind Hall A.

I could see Kendra and Tyrone sitting together on a bench near the swing set. Swinging on the swing set was a group of girls who liked to call themselves the "Cheetah Girls," after the popular movie of the same name. They behaved much like the girls in that movie. They matched outfits and hairstyles consistently and were sometimes catty. On this day, the girls stopped swinging and approached the twins. From where I was standing, I could only see the occasional hair flip and pointing of fingers. Then suddenly I saw Kendra was sobbing while running towards the hall with Tyrone at her heels.

I didn't see Kendra or Tyrone for the rest of the day. The following week I finally saw my friends as they snuck into the classroom like two snakes hiding from a hawk. Later that day, at lunch, surrounded by our classmates indiscreetly whispering and giggling, they finally told me what had happened on the playground. Our school's Cheetah Girls had called Kendra the forbidden n-word and told her that she did not belong in our community and on our playground because her skin was not white.

This was the moment when my eyes were truly opened to the realness of racial discrimination and the problems of race relations. Not much has changed since that day in fifth grade. Every day, situations arise like the one that I witnessed near the swing set, and I have personally seen instances of bigotry happen frequently throughout high school, college, and in my workplace. I have learned many lessons throughout my two decades of life, and one of the most important is that the color of one's skin does not determine what one can and cannot do or which playground one is allowed to play on.

PART II

The Police

SHANTERRIA
THE DIRTY SOUTH

The cool breeze of the night is blowing into your car as you ride with your music blasting through its speakers. You are in your car coming from a friend's house. You are a black female, and you have your black male friend along with you as you travel home. The energy is high, and you and your friend are feeling the vibes from each other as you ride home without a care in the world.

Suddenly, flashing red lights are behind you along with the sound of a siren you know all too well. Your vibe just got more intense and on edge as you hear and see what could be your decision in life. Your thoughts about your next move are being scrambled around in your head: What to do and where to go? Your heart pounds faster and faster as the minutes go by. You are driving in the darkness of the night, trying to find anyone who can see you besides your friend and the flashing lights and sirens that follow you. You pull over to what seems to be a good spot and wait for what comes next. You look at your mirrors and see a man get out of his car and approach you in your car.

You look forward, with both hands on the steering wheel, debating whether to stay calm or to go into your survival mode. Your friend looks at you, and then you both look forward without speaking a word. The man taps on the window as you still look forward, motionless, unable to process what is really taking place. He taps on the window for a second time, and it snaps you out of your train of thought. You calmly, making no sudden movements, roll down your glass to see what the problem is. The officer steps back from the car to get a good look at you as you roll down your window. "How may I help you, Officer?" you say. There is a moment of silence. You and the officer both look at each other: the officer judges you as you judge him.

"Step out of the car," the officer says, and just like that, your night could go anywhere.

DELISA

MY SOUL CRIED OUT

Baton Rouge. A city that is known for being the capital of Louisiana. A city that is known for Louisiana State University. A city that is known for its French history, along with other cities in Louisiana. A city that has its own music, unique slang, historical buildings, and art, among other things. A city that, if you travel to a certain parts of it, is torn down, full of homeless veterans and full of despair. The same city that is crowded during home games at LSU with people from all over the world. My city since 2012. The city that I grew to love. I came to Baton Rouge a year after I separated from the Navy. I did not want to stay home in Shreveport and saw better opportunities in the capital city. Like other cities, it's full of people from different places in life who have decided to be a part of its population. However, just as I discovered during my military service to this country, Baton Rouge is a city full of inequality and racism. Its name became part of a few hashtags in the summer of 2016. One hashtag was from a historic flood but mainly the hashtags of #AltonSterling and #PoliceBrutality.

July 5, 2016 was a month, a day of the week and year that someone would die and someone would be born. However, on this day Baton Rouge became more popular. My city did not become more popular because of a big football game at LSU or a celebrity shooting a movie in town. It became more popular because a black man, Alton Sterling, was shot and killed. I was in Shreveport at the time, and I got the call from one of my friends in Baton Rouge. After I heard the news, I went on to my Instagram account, and once again my heart skipped a beat just as it had so many times before when another man or woman of color was killed by the "protectors." Alton Sterling was not shot and killed because he did anything wrong. He was shot and killed because of the color of his skin. He was robbed. He was robbed of the life he was supposed to live. He is not able to do what he loved to do because of the color of his skin. He is not able to take care of his children because of the color of his skin. July 17, 2014 (Eric Garner, Staten Island, New York), August 9, 2014 (Michael Brown Jr., Ferguson, Missouri), November 22, 2014 (Tamir Rice, Cleveland, Ohio) . . . and the list goes on of the black men and women who have lost their lives to someone who leaves their spouse and kids each day to go out and "protect" their community.

So I ask, what is protection? Is it for a police officer to wake up and go out into the streets to take that man's life, that woman's life? A few of the black men and women who have become a part of a hashtag because of his or her skin color: #AltonSterling #TamirRice #TanishaAnderson #FreddieGray #SandraBland and the list goes on and on. I am restless. I am restless with this inequality, I am restless with this injustice. My soul is hurting, my people are hurting. What is a life to you? Each day a baby is born, and that child is expected to live a long and healthy life unless he or she arrives with complications. That same man or woman who was born now has to lie in a grave because his or her life was not valued by the people who chose to take it. So what is a life to you? Is it so lacking in value that watching the blood spill out onto the streets means nothing to you? Where is the justice? Where is the peace? Where is the love? Would there be love and peace if a man or woman who wasn't of color lay on the concrete after just being shot down? The injustice in this country is overwhelming. It should not take the hashtag #BlackLivesMatter and public protests for these killings to stop. It should not take a movement for these killings to stop.

So take a moment the next time you are around your mom, dad, son, daughter, cousin, friend. Take your hand and place it on the chest of a loved one; a loved one whom you love and depend on. Now imagine that loved one leaving home, never to return. Imagine never being able to feel their heartbeat, never being able to feel their warm skin. Never being able to feel their embrace, watch them graduate college, see their smile, hear their voice, taste their food, laugh with them. Imagine them being in a police altercation where they complied; their hands were raised, their hands were still. Now imagine them in a pool of blood because even after their hands were raised, even after they complied, they were still killed. Are you angry yet? Are you hurting yet? Do you see the value of life now? Let's not pretend that everyone is treated the same. Let's not pretend that the Black Lives Matter movement is not necessary. Let's stop pretending. Let's admit that if these men or women killed were not of color, they would be alive right now. Let's start to help. Let's start to bring more awareness. Let's start to speak. Let's start to give, let's start to love. What would you do if it was your child, your father, your mother? Would you speak up then?

I pray for a day of peace. I live for a day of true freedom and not freedom with bondage. Because my freedom is not free. It costs. It costs because I am different.

THE BOYS IN THE NEIGHBORHOOD

Walking to the neighborhood store was always fun for my friends and me. The popular store in my South Baton Rouge neighborhood had the best lemonade, hotdogs, nachos, and more. Occasionally, a couple of friends and I would meet at the neighborhood gym, shoot hoops, or just hang out. However, one day our trip to the corner store after school led to a disturbing encounter with police. Deep in conversation and laughter, we were enjoying walking the streets. Even though we were thinking of lemonade and junk food, the voices of our parents were always there, warning us to be careful of the Baton Rouge Police Department. They reminded us that too many of us were harassed for just walking.

It was a hot, humid day, so some of us had taken off our school uniform shirts. We always wore white or colored undershirts under our uniform shirts. We all lived in the neighborhood, so sometimes we would drop our book sacks at home before heading to hang out. When we made it to the store, we began to chat with the store owner. Though he was Nigerian, he always acted like he was from South Baton Rouge. South Baton Rouge has some rough areas, where many residents do not have a lot of education. However, he always encouraged us to finish school. After talking to him for a while, we headed for the exit.

As soon as we made it out the door, we noticed a couple of cop cars with siren lights on in the store's parking lot. I could see they had a few guys up against their cars, checking them for illegal possessions, I assumed. My dad had always told me to pay attention to feelings and signs when they are given. I knew one of the guys from around the neighborhood, and we sort of made eye contact in an acknowledging kind of way. One of the white officers saw and yelled to us, "All of you, hands on the car, now!" I remember thinking to myself, "Why the hell did I even look at that guy?"

After walking toward his unit, he made us place our store items on the ground. With his hand on his weapon, he yelled again, "Hands on the car, now!" Well, we did exactly as he said. I asked the officer in the politest way possible, "What did we do, Officer?" He replied bluntly, "Interfering with police business." We all looked at each other in shock. The officer began to pat us down; I think there were four of us. Though he started with one of my friends, I knew I would be next because I was on the side of him. He began yanking things out of my friend's pockets and throwing them to the ground. I was very frustrated with his actions and felt so much anger in my heart, so again I asked, this time a little more firmly, "What did we really do, Officer?"

The officer stopped searching my friend, turned to me, and yelled square in my face, "Hands on the f--king car, now!" He kicked both my legs apart to make them spread wider. I had on headphones which were attached to my iPod. Immediately, he snatched the headphones off my head, causing my iPod to slam to the ground. He began taking items out of my pockets; I had approximately $20 in ones. He threw the money to the ground, and I mumbled "You can't be serious." The officer then looked at me, grabbed me by the throat, and slammed my back against the hot hood of his car. While doing this he said, "Keep your f--king mouth closed, or next time it will be worse." I was so mad, an angry tear rolled down my face. Thankfully, a black officer intervened; I think his rank may have been higher. The black officer told us to gather our things and leave the premises immediately or get taken to jail. We hurried to collect our items and left the premises in disbelief about what had just happened.

Until that brief, violent encounter and the recent killings of many of black African American men, I had a lot of respect for police officers. Now, I was pretty uneasy with all colors of police officers after some cruel things I saw them do to people of color all across the world. Despite my own feelings, when I heard about the killings of two Baton Rouge police officers in July 2016, I didn't feel like justice was served. I was at home watching episodes of *Martin* when I heard about the police shootings. I initially thought it was an act of the government possibly trying to cover up something. My emotions were mixed, and I immediately began to pray, "Lord, let your will be done." No man or woman deserves to lose their life senselessly; that is not justice for African Americans.

JONATHAN

AMERICA ME

"Did you see what happened on Foster last night?" asked my wife through a text message, followed by a link. I will never forget that link she sent me. It wouldn't open on my phone, so I pulled it up on my computer. The graphic images that loaded onto my desktop screen showing what occurred between Alton Sterling and two officers of the Baton Rouge Police Department will be forever embedded in my memory. "Oh my God, oh my God, he just shot him!" These were the cries I heard being uttered by one of the voices behind the Instagram video that recorded two white police officers shooting and consequently murdering Alton Sterling while straddling him as he lay on the ground. After watching the video, I just closed the door to my office and cried in silence. From watching social media, the local and even national news, I could see that the outrage and controversy surrounding the shooting of Alton Sterling in Baton Rouge only fueled race tensions in America. It illustrated once again that, although we're in the year 2016, much has not changed since 1965. In 2001, my father was killed in our front yard by police, so I had witnessed this type of event firsthand. Watching the Alton shooting really opened up the fifteen-year wound, as if I was watching them gun down my father all over again.

I can remember as a child growing up in segregated Welsh, Louisiana; racism was very much alive. Growing up in Welsh meant that if you were black, the only thing you did with whites was go to school. Beyond school, blacks and whites hardly ever interacted with one another. Blacks stayed on their side of the tracks, and whites stayed on theirs. If a white person did happen to wander onto our side of the tracks, it was probably because they worked for the town of Welsh. If they didn't, they just got stares from neighbors, as if they were a Tyrannosaurus Rex taking a stroll down the street. The segregation of the two races is just the tip of the iceberg in my small hometown. In addition, to this day, the Klu Klux Klan is still openly active and operating in Welsh. As many know, the Ku Klux Klan is a secret society that focuses on white supremacy and terrorizes other races of people. They are especially known for terrorizing the African American race. Today, in the town of Welsh, the KKK still has rallies and public protests, its members still walk the streets, and they even still have cross-lighting ceremonies. Having this type of hate group still walking your neighborhood streets in 2016 shows just how separate and unevolved my hometown is.

I experience racism not only back in my hometown but also in my workplace. I had figured this would be the place where I would probably be the safest, with all of the laws set in place that do not allow for discrimination in the workplace. However, my foreman on my first job as a boilermaker was sitting at the lunch table playing with his pocketknife, and being the friendly natured person I am, I attempted to start a conversation with him. I said, "Man, it looks like your knife is kinda dull." His response to me was "I would cut your black ass, but I would hate to get shit on my knife." He then continued playing with his knife, as if what he said to me was not offensive. After that, I felt enraged by the utter disrespect, but because of my race, I had to weigh my options. Do I report him to the supervisor, who happens to be his best friend? Do I say what's on my mind, which may scare him but makes me the villain? Do I slap him for disrespecting me, a grown man, like that? When contemplating all of these options, I came to the conclusion that they either would lead to me being ostracized or fired without the chance of re-employment. I believe the fact that we are at work is the reason that foreman feels safe to say slick things like that to someone who is six inches taller, ten years younger, one hundred pounds bigger, and black. This is just a typical occurrence of racist things that are said when you are an African American in a predominantly white worksite.

Yet not all white people I have worked for or with are blatant racists. Some are subtle racists, like my ex-coworkers the Grahams. I worked with the father and his sons in many states and was treated like one of the family. They would literally do anything for me. They took me under their wing and taught me everything they knew about construction work, so much that I was able to accelerate my career faster than any other person with whom I started working. The Grahams took care of me. They made sure I had a job when I needed one. When the plant would lay off people, I could call the father, and he would make sure they had a spot for me.

The Grahams are from Mississippi, although they all worked in Louisiana. They would state frequently that they had a Mississippi mentality when it came to race. They truly believed that races should never mix. They believed blacks should only be with blacks and whites should only be with whites. Although they treated me like family, one day reality hit me, and I realized that no matter how comfortable I was or what they did for me, I was not one of them by any means. On the way to a job in Kentucky with Justin, the youngest of the Grahams, we had to stop at the father's home so that Justin and his dad could trade vehicles. Justin asked me to get his dad's keys out of the house, but when I got out of the truck, he said, "Oh, I forgot—never mind, Jonathan, I got it, don't worry about it." I thought that it was really weird because he had just asked me to get the keys, and all of a sudden he was like, "never mind." Then I remembered a conversation I'd had with Roland Sr., Justin's dad, a long time before. He told me "Jonathan, I'll always help you any way possible, but a black man will never step foot in my house. That is just the way I was raised, and the way I raised all my children." When he told me that, I was in shock. I thought, "This is the man whom I ask anything of and he helps me out whenever I need him." It was unbelievable then and still is to this day. When people say stuff like that to me, it leaves me stunned: how can you say something so prejudiced to another human being and be serious. Are you joking? I think momentarily, "This has to be a joke, because I would never tell another person this and be absolutely serious." On that day with Justin, I got back into the truck and waited for him to come out of the house with his father's keys. He soon did, we switched vehicles, and headed back out on the road. Soon after, he called his dad to tell him he dropped off his truck. His dad wanted to know if I had entered the house. After laughing it off, I asked Justin, "So your dad is serious about a black man not coming in his house?" All Justin said was, "Jonathan, my dad was born in the '50s in Philadelphia, Mississippi; that's how he was raised." I didn't respond; I just sat there stuck in silence in the passenger seat, looking out the window, just thinking.

The discussion of race in our country has always been a very sensitive subject, but a discussion is where we must at least begin in order to change this country so that African Americans can feel as though they have a place where they belong. We must fix the issue that African Americans are seen as the enemy or as inferiors. There is no need to be afraid of us simply because our skin is different. We have made a little progress over the last several decades with regard to race relations; however, it is clear that we still have a problem and no longer can we pretend that it doesn't exist. Only a genuine and earnest effort to address race relations within our country will fundamentally and honestly provide the overdue and necessary fix that our country needs.

TOMEKIA
A MELTING POT OF RACISM

In 1988, I was nine years old and had no clue that racism was alive and well. I was born to a biracial father and a mother who is of Trinidadian and Haitian descent. My grandmother whose skin was white as snow loved me with a love like no other love I had ever known. So, when I moved to my father's hometown of Franklinton, Louisiana, where my grandmother lived, I just naturally assumed that it would be a diverse and friendly area like the one I was accustomed to back home. I had no clue there was an unspoken rule in the town. On the playground one day, I was told by two girls whom I considered my friends that they could not play with me anymore because their dad told them whites don't play with "niggers." When I arrived home, I told my grandmother what happened to me. She explained that the n-word was used by bigots to hurt and belittle people but to pay no mind to that word because that could never be me. Although my grandmother's words were kind and healed my pain, the n-word stuck with me. This one event became the foundation for my views on race that took shape over time.

Time marched on in Franklinton, but the beliefs of the town stayed the same. The "whites only" pool was still there and was protected by private membership. I often wanted to swim there but was not allowed. Situations like this made me feel less of a person. Why was my skin not OK in this town? What about my skin made me not worthy of swimming next to the white kids? I would often ask why but would receive a response like, "That's just the way things are, and you have to accept it." At seventeen, this response was no longer enough for me. I longed for the day when Franklinton would be a distant memory.

I became a woman and made sure I married a black man. The reason for marrying someone black was not because of racism on my part. I saw what that town could do to biracial kids, and it was already hard just to be black. We raised our children in a town about twenty minutes away from Franklinton. We tried to protect them from the ugliness of racism, but that didn't last that long. This town of Bogalusa was the home of the Ku Klux Klan and still held on to their values of the Old South. I remember like yesterday coming home from work and stopping at a backwoods store to pick up a few items; there was the KKK in all their glory. My heart raced. I felt like that little girl on the playground again but with so much more fear. Then I heard, "Nigger, it is night and you better get out of here." I still don't remember the drive home; fear had put me in a state of shock. When I arrived home, my husband saw the fear on my face and in that moment we both agreed it was time to move.

Baton Rouge was the city we chose to finish raising our children and build a new life. We chose this city because of its diversity and the opportunities for our children to have a better education than we did. Back home we had to worry about our neighbors' frowns because we were living in *their* neighborhood, or we had to worry about their child saying something racist to our children. The police were never a concern, mainly because we had attended school together since early childhood. However, in Baton Rouge, the police were no small-town cops, and they fully enforced the law.

After living in Baton Rouge for five years, I had my first en-counter with the police. My son Trevionne and his friend, who at that time were fifteen, were threatened by another boy with a gun. Trevionne stopped a police officer because his father and I had told him police were there to protect him. He told the officer what had happened to them. Instead of listening to the boys, that offi-cer ordered them to get into the back of the police car and made them point out where the child with the gun lived. The officer then knocked on the door and informed the boy's mother that my child was accusing her child of having a gun. Trevionne called me from his cellphone in fear and said, "Mom, I am in the back of a police car. This boy threatened me with a gun." His next words were, "Mom, I am scared. His mother is pulling on the door trying to confront me."

I ran out of my job and rushed to my baby boy. When I arrived, I asked the officer why he put my child in danger like that. His response was, "These boys do this all the time, and there probably wasn't a gun."

I responded, "Well, aren't you going to do something about this child and his mother's actions?"

He replied, "There is nothing to be done here."

I asked him what made him think he had the right to order these boys into the back of the car and force them to face their attacker? In return, I received no response, just a blank stare. How could he think he was justified in ordering juveniles who had done nothing wrong—and without the consent of their parents—to con-front their aggressor? I asked for his badge number, and he said it quickly as if I was annoying him. Then he got in his car and drove away just as fast as he could.

I cried that night at home in bed because in telling my son that police were there to protect him I had put him in an unsafe situa-tion. We raised our son to respect police officers. We told him they were the good guys. Did I tell him the wrong thing? Did I fail my child? After that day, we told our son that if anything happens, to just come home and Dad will take care of the rest. "Do not stop the police again, son. We need you home and safe." How does a parent go from teaching that police are protectors to instructing children not to talk to them? For a while, I wondered if we told our son the right thing. A few months later, we realized the fear we had was justified, and something much worse can happen to young black men by the people sworn to protect them.

In July 2016 I watched the video once, twice, then a third time. This has got to be a hoax, I thought. Then the comments appeared on the news feed. Someone was really losing his life as a camera rolled. The video showed a man being tased, and then they showed cops struggling to get him on the ground. Once he was on the ground, one officer restrained the bottom of his body, including his arms. The other officer was restraining the top half. While this was going on, this man had a look of confusion on his face. The next thing I heard was "He has got a gun," and there was a struggle. He was still subdued after the struggle, but then I saw the officer fire his gun. I do feel those officers had some fear. I wondered, "Was the fear solely the situation at hand, or did it come from the presumption in this country that black men are a menace and something to be feared?" This puzzled me, because I could clearly see the man in the video was being held down on the ground. I was in disbelief. How could this really be happening right here in Baton Rouge? I later learned his name was Alton Sterling. He was a black man, a father, someone's son, and a friend to many in his community but on this day, he was treated as a criminal, though he was merely selling CDs. In my eyes, then and now, Alton Sterling, was a victim.

ZACHARY

THE INNOCENCE OF A CHILD

I n the summer of 2016 I worked in a plant as a scaffold build-
er. Before starting the job, I did not realize how many black
men were employed there. I was a tall skinny white kid who had
just turned eighteen, working in the middle of a mostly black
plant; it was a little intimidating. I was not scared of anyone, but
I was by myself. I was the minority. After a little while, one of
my coworkers took me under his wing. He showed me around,
introduced me to the other workers, and made me feel less of
an outcast.

His name was Leo. He was only twenty-two, so it was perhaps
easier for him to relate to me than for the older guys. As we were
working one day, he told me, "You know, you're one of the only
white kids who doesn't piss me off. I almost feel like your older
brother. I'll cut up with you and all, but if you screw up, or say some
dumb shit, you better believe that I'll be on your ass all day." After
he said that, I told him, "Yeah, and same to you. But don't think
just because you're older than me that I won't get on your ass just
as well." He laughed and told me to get back to work.

I finally started getting into a routine. I would arrive at the
parking lot for 5 a.m. and take the bus into the plant. Regardless

of the time, we would always joke around on the bus. For instance, whoever sat in the front seat got control of the radio and would sometimes put on what he thought would most get on the nerves of the rest of us. I quickly found out that so-called smooth jazz was music that nobody else favored but me.

After we all started getting along, something drastic happened. A black man by the name of Alton Sterling was shot and killed point blank by a Baton Rouge police officer. I found out that same night, and instantly thought about the next day. What will the black workers think about what happened? What will they say to me, the only white guy in the crew? Would they think that somehow I had something to do with it, or that because I'm white, I should take responsibility for what a white police officer has done? I was right to anticipate mistrust.

When I got on the bus the next morning, not one person said a single word to me. They didn't even make eye contact with me. It was as though it was my first day on the job again, and no one knew who I was. I thought to myself, I was working in the plant just like all of you, yet you still try to blame me for what the police did? For the most part, nobody really said too much about it to me. They would ask me what I thought about it, or if I'd watched the video, but nothing too serious. As the days went on and the Black Lives Matter activists started protesting, the men at the plant decided they wanted their voices heard as well. Since I was the only white guy in the crew, they came to me.

Once we got on the bus, it was as if the blinders came off. They started joking about me being the cop's son and claiming that I would do the same thing if I ever got the chance. They then stated that they should bring me to the rallies, shouting that they had a white kid, and urge the other protesters to beat me with bats and hang me like the slave owners did to the slaves. Or that maybe I should get beaten and tased while two men held me down, while I tried not to move.

I tried not to get involved with the men's reactions too much. I just wanted to keep my mouth shut, make my money, and go home. I tried not to let any of their slanders affect me, but after a while I was overcome with a slight depression. Going to sleep became more difficult to do. I could almost see the black protesters chasing after me. As much as I would tell them that I had nothing to do with it, it was as if it went in one ear and out the other. For a second, I almost started believing that I actually was involved in it somehow.

When six policemen in Baton Rouge were shot, and three died, a couple of weeks later, I could not fathom how people thought killing innocent police officers was going to resolve the issue. In fact, it made it incredibly worse. I am not saying that killing Alton Sterling was right in any way, but those police officers did not shoot him just out of revenge. I was angry, but frightened at the same time. I did not know if blacks were mad at just the police officers or at white people altogether. I felt like I had to stay on my guard at all times, not knowing if something was going to break out wherever I went.

Hearing about the shootings, I could not believe how close they were to home. You hear about tragedies happening in other states: for instance, when Michael Brown was shot in Ferguson, Missouri. When it happens only twenty minutes up the road, it makes living in that city surreal. You can't help but feel empathy for the families involved in the tragedies. I felt helpless knowing I couldn't do anything to help, except to think about how racism gets a hold of us. Society puts a chip in our brains, telling us how to see or how we should act. Eventually, we start to listen to it, not because it is right, but because nobody is telling us it is wrong. Why is it that because of a difference in color, we have to act differently around each other, or be afraid of each other, or even kill another?

Growing up as a child, I was more worried about my friends as people, rather than the color of their skin. I did not see black, white, Mexican, or Asian. I saw another friend on the playground. It was not until I started getting older that I started seeing color, only because society had put labels on everyone. Just imagine how different the world would be if we could all revert back to our childhood when it comes to race: a time when being a different color didn't mean you should be picked last, or that you are any greater or any lesser than the person beside you. Seeing someone who is a different race from you shouldn't scare you off, but rather invite you in to learn more about their different cultures and even struggles.

JACOSIE

DID YOU EXPERIENCE IT?

On May 20, 2003, I started going to day care at Little Bees Day Care in Baker, Louisiana. It was an all-white day care. My mom had begun to fill out my paperwork when a white parent walked through the door and approached the day care nurse. "Are you all letting this nigga attend here? You all must accept childcare assistance." The day care nurse stated, "Yes, we are accepting her, and no, we do not accept childcare assistance. It's still $175 a week." My mom looked up but she just ignored them and told me, "Don't mind her." Surprisingly, as my mom continued to do my paperwork, a little white kid stuck her tongue out at me and laughed. I immediately thought to myself that white people are dirty. I was registered and my mom paid my money. She handed me my lunch bag and said, "Don't worry about them kids; just have fun." I replied, "OK, Mom."

As the day went on, I sat by myself with no one to play with or talk to. Was it because their parents said something? I started to cry and wondered why no one wanted to play with me. Was it because I'm black? The teachers were the only nice people, but not the kids. I tried to ask the teachers what the problem was, but they always told me I was too young to understand. When it was time for lunch, I had my own food that my mom had prepared. A white girl with green eyes, blonde hair, and two ponytails said, "That black girl thinks she is special." I always wondered why they called me "that black girl" and not Jacosie. Was it because they did not know how to pronounce my name or because their parents told them to call black kids "black"? It was then nap time and I went to get my mat from my cubby. A girl with long black hair pushed me. I began to get very upset, and I attacked her. When it was time to go home, my mom came to get me, and I told her what had happened at day care. She told me, "Baby girl, keep your head up. White people look at us like dogs." Those days of being bullied at daycare were harsh. As I look out now at the world we live in, with all this racial profiling and killing, I think back to Little Bees day care and see a connection to the killing of Alton Sterling.

I will never forget the night Alton Sterling was murdered, held down by two white cops. My boyfriend and I left the very store where the killing took place after we talked to Alton himself. As we pulled away, we saw the police cars approach the store; we weren't thinking that they were coming to take an African American male's life. On our way home, Alton's aunt called my boyfriend and said, "Them white bitches killed my nephew." What if we had still been there? Would they have shot my boyfriend? Or maybe even both of us? I did not know how to comfort my boy-friend right then; Alton was someone he knew growing up. To get that phone call hurt. When we reached home, I sat down and told him "Babe, watch yourself around these police. They are dirty, and I don't need you to be one of their victims." Although the protest that followed Alton's killing was a good idea, I don't feel it was done right because it led up to more violent events. Those events resulted in a black man getting killed in his car by a police-man and six police officers getting shot, three of them killed. I thought to myself, What is this world coming to? Is the violence going to get worse?

As a parent of a three-month-old baby boy, I wonder if it will be hard for my son to live in this world. Will he be threatened by police because of the color of his skin? Will whites harass him? Even though he is only three months, I always tell him, "Son, you are a handsome black male, and don't let no one tell you different." I feel scared about how—and where—I am going to raise him. Should I move? Will life be better elsewhere? Is life the same? When he goes to school, will it be safe? Since Alton's death, I keep recalling the racist kids at Little Bees Day Care. I do not want that treatment for my son. I want him to be able to play with whites and blacks, not just his race. When I was pregnant, I never thought about how I had to raise my son in this environment—not until the day he was born. It hit me then that I had an African American baby boy who would have be raised around all this negativity.

My thoughts on race relations are that people follow what they were told when they were growing up or what they have seen. This racist violence has gotten out of control in the city of Baton Rouge. I feel we need to come together as a community to solve this issue. Everyone should be treated equally; no one should look at someone differently based only on race. We Baton Rouge residents should put what we were taught when we were raised behind us and start over. Blacks and whites should come together and unite as one.

CHARLES

COPS IN THE BLACK COMMUNITY

I grew up in South Baton Rouge. Growing up there, you only worried about stray bullets and cops. Even the music from around my neighborhood told the stories of run-ins with dirty cops. There were two cops who bothered everyone in my neighborhood more than any others. They would often pull a car over to harass the driver, even if the person was going the speed limit and nothing was wrong with the car. And they would stop people walking down the street to do pat downs. They even harassed my uncle and while doing so, told my mother to "shut the f--k up" or they'd arrest her, too. I already didn't like cops, and that experience made my feelings toward them worse.

As I became older, I heard, and even saw on the news, more stories about the negative ways cops treat people of color. Even the music around that time told of the way dirty cops treated people. During Black History Month, we learned about older stories of almost the same sort. Though things are somewhat better now, they still aren't perfect. It hurts to know someone who is supposed to serve and protect you could hate the sight of you. I remember going to sleep loathing polices officers. To me, they became the worst people alive. I didn't like talking to them and hated being around them. There are police who are supposed to enforce the law but don't follow the law themselves, and they get away with murder by saying they feel threatened.

However, about two years ago, I changed my mind about cops. One would come by when my cousins and I were playing basketball. He would stop and play with us for a while. We had something in common. I felt that they usually put cops who couldn't and wouldn't try to relate to a community in our neighborhoods. This one was different. People who have something in common often get along better than people who don't.

That's why the relationship between cops and the residents of predominantly black neighborhoods are usually bad or nonexistent. That's why incidents like the Alton Sterling and Philando Castile shootings keep happening. Despite the negative actions of police, I do not support the police killings that have happened. Murder is murder. How many people must lose their lives before we realize more hate isn't going to solve anything? That we can only solve things by talking and coming to a mutual understanding?

ALL LIVES MATTER

I have always grown up in a small town where there were not many African American around. Growing up hearing the words that my family, and friends and even words I would say that are not appropriate. Blacks think they are being targeting in this mess, but to me it is all people and their acts to police. Police are protecting us and risking their lives to be better and live easier; they deserve respect. When you get pulled over, or checked by the police, all you would have to do is obey them and cooperate. Cooperation will make them pleased with you and it will also make your time dealing with them shorter and easier. To me, it needs to be "All lives matter." As a Christian, I believe everyone is a son of God, no matter your color.

Growing up in Clinton, Louisiana, I did not really hangout or talk to African Americans. My small town and family never really had African Americans in our daily routine, they were around and I noticed the difference between us. The things my dad and others are always saying, the things they do about African Americans; growing up hearing that made it second nature to me so of course I grew the habit. I knew it was a bad thing, but the way I grew up around it seemed impossible to get out of that. I finally escaped the habit because one of my best friends came around when I was in middle school. When he was around he seemed like a brother to me. It felt so natural. I never thought of my best friend coming over to my house. When I invited him to my home, it was like my parents had to switch their attitudes. In my parent's perspective, African Americans are a negative influence. My best friend showed my parents that no matter your color, we are all the same. We are all human.

African Americans think they are being targeted in everything that has been going on. Some think that the fix is to shoot and try to exterminate cops. It is not just African Americans; it is all ethnic groups committing crimes as awful as this. The real reason behind the civilians getting shot is because they are putting the cop's life in danger. The cops are just trying to protect themselves. To me, if everyone would respect and listen to one another, we will all return home safely to our families. The police's main goal is to protect and serve civilians, but this cannot happen without the society's respect and cooperation.

Cops have one of the toughest jobs. Having to protect a city, parish, or state is a lot to handle. Having a family only makes it harder to endure. It puts more stress on the family having to worry about the loved one on the job. Personally, if one of my parents were to be an officer the only thing I would worry about is their safety. Officers are here to protect, not to hurt. Officers will do what need to be done to protect themselves and society. The officers have recently had their lives taken because of protesting that had gone out of hand. Lives have also been taken because of uncooperative people. Even things as simple as traffic violations can turn wrong because people don't listen or they don't want to face consequences. So, they try and run or shoot the officer.

Our world today is far away from normal with all the racism and bad things going on. The main events today are the killing of cops and protesting. To make this better, we need to stop fighting and come together. To me, the only way we are going to get over this is realizing we have all made mistakes. Also, I believe we all need to make up before something bad as another Civil War occurs. We all need to trust in God and believe he knows what is best for us. It is evident that fighting and tension is not the solution.

KACI

THE APOLOGY

During a relatively short day, I sat down to check my Facebook as usual. A few notifications, some messages, and a friend request or two: nothing seemed out of the ordinary. As I glanced unenthusiastically over the trending topics, nothing caught my eye: Kevin Durant leaves Oklahoma, uproar over the Trump versus Clinton, the first Lois Lane dying at age 85. Nothing really seemed too jaw-dropping at first glance; it was just a bunch of names I either didn't know or didn't care about. As I scrolled through my timeline, I did see an occasional cop body cam video, but thinking things were finally settled about past incidents like Sandra Bland, Eric Garner, Michael Brown, or Trayvon Martin, I decided to ignore it. As long as things were right and people received their justice, that's all that mattered. As I kept going, though, I'd see pictures of a man showing up on occasion, all from the same three people out of the few hundred I am friends with. Confused and concerned, I looked more into what was going on. I wasn't prepared for the information that I found as I continued.

This man, Alton Sterling, was younger than my father. He had five children. He had a complicated past, but that wasn't known at the time of his death. Being from a small town, most people I know have a questionable past (drunk driving or drug use, and everything in between). What if this was my father? What if this was my mother?

As I try to explain the stories to people from my area, I get so many mixed responses: from "I can't believe what this world has come to" to "He probably deserved it; most of them are good for nothing anyway." That lays heavily on my heart. Because of prejudice against the race and gender of another person, labels like "good for nothing" and "criminal" are made.

When Facebook asked me if I was safe during the protests, I pondered, Am I safe? Are my friends safe? What I've established is that, no, I'm not safe. We, as a community, as a country, are not safe. As people are mauled and killed for standing up for themselves, for living their normal lives, how can we as a whole be safe?

I, like many others, just assume that things like the shooting of an innocent person aren't a problem in my area. It's an isolated incident. These things happen somewhere else, somewhere not close to home. I say, "This can't be my town." I believe that, at least until my friend gets pulled over with a full car of people. As the police try to persuade the people in the back that they are not willingly in the car, my friend is threatened to be arrested. Would I be this unlucky if I weren't a white woman? Do I have to constantly get updates on my friends who aren't part of the majority just so I can sleep soundly, knowing that they are safe for the moment?

Why aren't we all rallied behind this? What are we doing and where have our morals all gone? Why, instead of supporting every community or man, are we justifying wrongdoing? Why are people saying that the victims deserve things like this, when all evidence proves otherwise? So many individuals are determined to say that oppression and persecution don't exist on a large scale. If it is so hard to look at with an entire race, let's put it on a smaller scale.

If anyone I know tells me that they are being abused or mistreated, who am I to tell them otherwise? Who am I to say that they are making it up? I'll stand by them no matter what. I'll be there for them, and I will support them through everything. Now throw this on a larger scale, and suddenly it's problematic? An entire group of people are being mistreated, but it isn't real, and it's all for attention? Why are we willing to stand for one but not for many? If someone showed up to a doctor's office concerned that he has cancer, would you turn him away? Or would you search high and low, examine him entirely, and bring in specialists to make sure that there is absolutely no problem? You wouldn't tell that person he is making up his problems with cancer, so why do it in the case of cancerous actions?

This community that we love has expressed an indescribable fear for their lives. How dare we tell them that their fears are unimportant? Racism, especially to this extent, is not a natural idea. It is completely learned from inconsiderate people to be suspicious of other people who aren't like you.

Responding with violence isn't the answer. This world is torn. We have to share love. We have to share respect. We have to get justice for everyone. We have to stand up and show that we are one. We must stand strong before this town is nothing but smoldering embers of problems past.

To the black community: I apologize. I apologize if I have ever been arrogant. I'm sorry if I ever spoke lies about your community or didn't seem to care enough about your feelings or your fears. If I have played any role in your persecution to make you feel like your voice isn't heard, I ask for your forgiveness.

My opinion on the Black Lives Matter protests does not matter. Neither does your opinion; it is irrelevant to the cause. This is too major to joke about. Instead of saying that you aren't racist, how about we stop those who are? We must step down from the clouds and look at the lives that are affected. We must look for a solution that brings us all together as a whole. We must remove this tumor of racism that is plaguing our community.

We must come together, to run the hatred out of the world and to love in the way that Christ loved us. We must allow the love to grow from our hearts into our area, and spread outward like a wildfire. Instead of speaking words, we must use our actions and stand up. Use our tongue that speaks life and death to protect our fellow brothers. We all aspire to be heroes, but when the time comes for us to serve our community, we run and hide. We must change the world, and if that involves starting in our own homes, our own streets, and our own towns, then let us go forth.

ZACHARY

LIVING IN A WORLD AS ONE

When I was in grade school, in social studies class we watched videos and learned about the civil rights movement. I grew up in a neighborhood where I didn't see any black people except when they mowed our lawn, though some went to school with me, which I thought was odd. I was curious as to why the only people I saw mowing the lawn were black and Mexican. My father told me when I was little boy that black people were the filthiest of them all; it made no sense why someone would tell a little boy that. As I got older, I started to realize that the tensions between the races were only getting worse as time went on.

Recently, in 2016, there were shootings of police officers and by police officers. There have been riots because of the shootings. When I heard about the shootings of the officers, I just couldn't believe what I was witnessing. One shooting particularly caught my attention. From what I heard, the officer aimed his gun at the black man; the black man informed the officer that he was armed and that he had a license to carry. The officer told him not to move, but the man told the officer that he was going to reach for his wallet; then the cop started shooting. I try to look at both sides: the cop shot the man because, I think, in his mind, even though the black man said he was armed and told him that he was going to reach for his wallet, the cop didn't trust him; the cop thought he was going to reach for his gun and shoot him. At the time, I couldn't believe what I was witnessing and listening to. I have struggled to live in a racial environment that I could not wrap my head around. That was the motivation that drove me to overcome, which made my faith stronger. I pushed and pushed myself day by day. That allowed me to have belief for the people who are going through obstacles, those who are pushing themselves to be better persons.

I was in my room surfing through my news feed when I first came across the shooting of Alton Sterling. My eyes widened more and more as I read about the horrible death of this innocent man. I ended up finding the video on Facebook. It was also on the news. When I found out what had happened, I had to sit down to process what was going on. It seemed crazy that this was going on in Baton Rouge. My emotions were going all over the place. I started to pace back and forth. I was really upset knowing that this happened where I go shopping. Right after that happened, I was scared to go to Baton Rouge to be honest with you. There were riots and more shootings going on in Baton Rouge. I just stayed home feeling helpless and continued to watch and listen to reports of what was going on just a couple miles away from me.

The relations between my race and other races has not been positive. We, who are white, are labeled to be all full of ourselves; the other races label us as thieves and just completely ruthless people. But I get along with anybody. I have all kinds of friends: black friends and Mexican friends. Judging by what went on in the summer of 2016, everyone protects their own kind as a natural defensive mechanism. But this reaction makes us feel that a war has begun, because that's how it happens.

I think the whole human race—and I mean every race—should unite to find some peace and start building bridges. Now it is not going to be that easy. We just need to take one step at a time. We need to shake hands with one another and live as one. We need to keep moving forward and never look back. We just need to keep believing and having faith. Eventually, we will make the world better for all races. I end this with a quote by John Lennon: "You may say I'm a dreamer, but I'm not the only one. I hope someday you'll join us, and the world will live as one."

CARLA

DIFFERENCES IN THE AGES

I was born and raised in the '70s in Columbia, Mississippi, where everyone knew everybody. There was not a lot of racial tension, and I think this was because our parents and teachers were more involved than they are today. I don't remember being told that I could not play or talk to anyone because of their skin color. We only cared about playing with our friends, and it did not matter to us where they were from or what color they were. We had parents, teachers, and friends who influenced us more than outside sources like television and social media. Our parents worked hard to instill in us morals and values along with the expectation of working hard for things in life. By the time I was in high school, though, things started changing. The black kids started blaming the white kids for slavery, which made no sense to me. I mean, my family never owned slaves and none of them had ever been slaves. In a way, I could understand where they were coming from, but their argument with me seemed pointless. I was always taught growing up that if you want something, then you should work for it and to treat people the way you would want to be treated. I still live by that teaching, and I have tried to instill those beliefs in my children as well. Twenty-four years ago, I was pregnant with my second child when I moved to Baton Rouge. I never pointed out skin color to my children; I tried to teach them to be open and accepting to all. I believe the increase of racial tension stems from lack of parenting, along with the government and media interference.

Over the past ten years or so, things have been getting increasingly worse between all races. Are parents teaching their children to hate others, or are parents just not involved and letting the world teach them? One Sunday last year, in 2016, my pastor preached about the importance of fathers and their hands-on participation in child raising. He made the point that all communities—not just white or black, but all—are struggling with the day-to-day challenges of raising children without a present father. Could this be a reason why the racial battle seems to have grown into a full-blown war? It could be a huge factor when the men these children look up to are rap artists, actors, and all around illusions of what men should be instead of father figures. However, this does not excuse the behavior of anyone. We have a problem when people do not want to take responsibility for their actions and instead blame others for the way their lives have turned out. We have too many people who think they are entitled because of their skin color, race, or circumstances from being a certain way.

However, we cannot blame tense race relations on any one race because instead of confronting the racial battle together, we have allowed current issues to divide us and set us back decades. Do our current media help to solve the race wars or make them worse with their taunting? For example, in the case of Alton Sterling's shooting, many in the media deemed the cops guilty of police brutality by watching a part of a video. What happened there is still a mystery because the media was more concerned with ratings instead of getting down to the truth. From all these recent shootings in 2016, the Black Lives Matter movement has done more damage to the race wars than anything else could have. They throw fits like a two-year-old who does not get his way, while burning down whole cities, attacking innocent people, and doing millions of dollars in damage all while blaming others. They go off half-cocked without any real proof of wrongdoing, and they are no better than the Ku Klux Klan or other white supremacists. Every one of them are racist groups that love to cause problems with other races.

Moreover, the current government does nothing to help reduce the tension because it seems to enjoy a country divided. From the press releases done for the multiple shootings to the "Great Flood" in August in Louisiana, it seems that the media and government are doing more harm than good. There has been no sign of the government trying to make the race wars better. For example, during the flood, they talked more about New Orleans and how residents there were doing when that city was not even affected. The president did a press release as hundreds of people were rescuing or being rescued, and the only thing he had to say was not to make it about race. We were not making anything about race. White crews were saving black families, and black crews were saving white families; the flood was not a race issue at all.

Is there any hope for a change to start building relationships, or are we doomed to continue to undo everything that people like Martin Luther King Jr. and Rosa Parks staked their lives on working towards? The sooner everyone decides that it is not a race problem but a heart problem that is causing the decrease in sense, the sooner things will get better. The sooner men and women step up and take responsibility for themselves, their actions, and their families, the better we will be. When the country decides that it is time to turn back to God and stop letting the devil divide us, things will improve. The government and media need to stay out of issues, local and foreign, that do not concern them. Parents need to stand up and feel free to be parents without the fear of repercussions when they discipline their children. Kids need to be taught that their actions have consequences. Schools need to teach the whole history and not what their teachers or the government deems fit. Families need to feel free to praise God and teach about him without the fear of public criticism. We need to take the values this country was founded on and extend them to everyone and not restrict them to the few the forefathers thought deserved full rights. America was made to be a free country, but so many are put into a sense of slavery by not being able to be who they are because of other people and their issues. It is time to stand up and say "Enough is enough" and not put up with it any longer. White people need to be done feeling bad for what their ancestors did, and black people need to rise above the things that their ancestors had to do. White people need to take credit only for what they have done and not for everyone else's problems. Until we stand up and quit letting others fill us with hate or the government and media dictate how we should live, we will continue to kill each other, harass each other, and blame each other for our problems.

THOMPSON

A FALSE REALITY

Have you ever seen one of those movies where there is a family always on the move? That was my childhood: almost every year a new house, friends, school, and neighborhood. As you might guess, it was hard in more ways than one. The one thing I didn't like was changing schools because every class had a joker. That was the only problem I had, and I tried to ignore them. The more time passed, the more they would make me angry. But I never had a problem making friends. The fact was, I was a lot smarter and wiser than the rest of my class. So I would use that knowledge to make friends who I could trust until, eventually, I stopped trying to because it didn't make any sense when I was going to move anyway.

By the time I was in 4th grade, we had moved four times.

However, when we moved during my fourth-grade year, I stayed at the same school, and I was happy about that. I had made a name for myself. I would beat the crap out of anybody who tried to bully me. It started out as self-defense. One fight was with a class clown. To be honest, I kind of liked it. After the fight, I was surprised to see how he acted towards me: he stopped making jokes about me, and he even started acting respectful. Seeing the fight and the way the dude was acting afterwards, everyone said I had won. The next thing I knew, every bully and comedian wanted to fight me. After a while, they were all scared of me, seeing as how I never lost a fight.

After a few fights, everyone kept their distance from me, and my family didn't understand me. I started doing the only thing I could do to escape my reality: dream. Why? Because dreams are places where you control the world, the rules, laws, and everything else. I started off sleeping; then I learned to daydream. I got so good, you couldn't tell if I was awake or asleep. I literally slept through most of elementary and middle school. Daydreaming was a good way to escape reality, but the problems were still there, plus my grades were suffering. So I started to look at the world as it was and not how I wanted it to be because just daydreaming was not going to help solve my problems. Sometimes, I would fall asleep without even knowing it; I decided I needed to face reality. The only thing I was doing was running and hiding from my problems.

When people ask me what my view on racism is, I say, "I don't have one." To be honest, I think of people as people. I don't see color or religion as a factor in what makes them who they are. White or black—hell, anyone can steal your phone, regardless of color or sex. I have never seen a case of racism, and don't see the shooting of Alton Sterling as being racist. The police station got a call about a man wearing a red shirt and selling CDs. The man had threatened a homeless man with a gun. Officers Blane Salamoni and Howie Lake II were sent to the scene to see what was going on. They saw a man who matched the description they were given and also saw that the man had a gun. They thought it was best to check if it was their man later. They were trying to make the arrest when Sterling dropped the gun. Thinking he was trying to draw the gun, they pinned him to the ground. The problem was the fact that Alton was still resisting which was why he was shot. This makes sense because people don't think straight when they are afraid.

Simple misunderstandings like this are a problem, but stupid things like revenge make it even worse. The 2016 shooting of

Dallas police officers, which killed five and left nine injured, is an example of this. Things like that make problems like police brutality more likely. There is a saying that "Bad blood leads to bad blood," which means that violence leads to more violence. So what happened next after the shooting of Alton Sterling were riots with more blood. I personally think racism does exist, but people just have it mostly all in their heads and try a lot of times to make something of nothing.

An article published in July 2016 in *The Daily Wire*, "7 Statistics That Show 'Systemic Racism' Doesn't Exist in Policing," says that a college student studied police shootings between 2000 and 2015, and of all these shootings, only 20 percent of the victims were black, while most were white. The study also showed that blacks are not over-arrested. The saying "People are blind to reality and only see what they want to see" is relevant here. What this means is that even if there is nothing, they will see something.

Growing up I went from school to school, and at every school I attended, there was a mixture of races and diverse religions. There was no racism throughout the schools. In school, there was conflict, like fighting, but this had nothing to do with color or religion. In the Constitution, the founding fathers said that "All men are created equal." Yet we all treat each other like we are so different, though we all eat, live, and die the same.

There is no reason why racism should exist in the first place. Racism is something that is quite simple and easy to avoid. People should act according to how they want to be treated. The reason why I personally have never experienced racism is because I act and do unto others as I would have them do unto me. I treat others with respect, and they do the same with me. Racism is something that will forever exist as long as people are blind to the truth and don't learn to accept what they see.

WE ARE MORE ALIKE

I was fortunate in my childhood that I didn't encounter racial problems. Some of my best friends then were black, and the same is true today. We are all alike and equal. That idea is forgotten when people judge others based on their skin and not on who they truly are; it is a serious problem in today's society. We should not judge people until we truly know them.

I grew up in Belle Rose, Louisiana, a little town right outside of the city of Donaldsonville, Louisiana, where the majority of people were white. I knew a few black kids and, believe it or not, our parents liked each other and so did we. We were all very good friends and still are. We would hang out together, play ball together, and do all sorts of activities together. We never had a problem with racism at school, at home, or on the field. Our neighbor was black, and we never had any problems. His sons used to come play at my house, or we would go across the street and play basketball at my cousin's house. The only thing I was ever told about race was that there are just as many bad black people as bad white people. I believe where I grew up had a big impact on how I think about different races because we never had any problems with anybody.

During seventh grade, our school took in underprivileged kids, and most of them were black. The reason most of these newcomers were black is because most of the white people were privileged and had money. I was always a privileged kid, so when this happened, I realized how fortunate I was. My family and friends helped out those unprivileged kids, and the color of their skin or where they came from didn't matter. As we moved on to high school, I became closer friends with some of those kids, and if they needed a ride to and from school or some school supplies, my family was always willing to help. Some of my white friends and I would bring black kids to school every day because they either didn't have a parent to bring them or didn't have a vehicle. If we went to McDonald's or Subway after school, I would offer to pay for their food because I knew they were struggling. If I asked them to help me or do something for me, they did; and if they asked me to do something for them, I did. So, when people say all whites are racist, I take offense because I am white and not racist.

I was at home in my living room watching the news when I heard that a white police officer killed a black man in Baton Rouge whose name was Alton Sterling. I turned and looked at my dad and said, "I bet people will riot and cause chaos because a white cop shot a black man, and people will think that the incident was racist because a white cop killed a black man." My dad responded "Yeah, you're probably right, and you know what is a shame? Some people will think that we are racist just because we are white, and some white people will be afraid that they will get harmed because they are white." He also said, "The news and social media is promoting the violence by giving the riots attention." I believe what he was saying was right. Social media sites need to realize that when they show racist things, it creates or adds to tension between races. I have been wondering why the news only shows black people getting shot by police and not white people, even though white people get shot, too. It's almost like the news is promoting racism.

The killing of police officers two weeks later was totally un-called for. They put their lives on the line to save the lives of others. Taking police lives is totally wrong and stupid. I feel sorry for the families who had to suffer for someone else's actions. I have a friend who is a cop; he is white and serves in the city of Donaldsonville. He said, "When I go to the gas station, people call me a 'pig' and spit on my shoes." How would you feel if someone did that to you because of someone else's actions? I know I would feel nervous everywhere I went in a police uniform. People need to stop looking at skin color and start looking at who each person really and truly is.

LAJERRICA
BLACK LIVES MATTER!

When I was in middle school, kids talked about how dark my skin was. I laughed and shrugged off their comments because I thought I was tough enough. When I got home and looked at myself in the mirror, it was a different story. I felt so disgusted with my appearance that I started to believe the kids at school. I always imagined what my life would be like if my skin were lighter because people who had light skin would get all the attention.

I remember when my P.E coach picked two students and told them to select who they wanted on their teams. I was always one of the bottom two, which made me feel like I was beneath others. I hated to be in the same room with some kids because they made me feel like I didn't belong. My father would always ask me, "Do you have a boyfriend?" I would reply back with a simple "no." In the back of my mind, I would be thinking about how the boys in my school didn't even look my way. Sometimes, I would secretly cry in my room because I felt so ugly and unattractive that I just gave up. However, it wasn't just my own race that made me feel bad about my skin color.

Some people actually believe that black folks don't belong here because our skin doesn't match theirs, or our hair is more natural than others, or our lips too big, or our ears too large, or because we weren't raised in upscale neighborhoods with big houses surrounded by green grass and a white picket fence. They believe that we don't belong here because our parents couldn't afford for us to go to private schools that have a golf course outside for kids to play on during their lunch breaks. It becomes tiresome when you're always put in a demeaning category.

EDUCATION BASED ON INEQUALITIES

I remember my parents always saying racism was a terrible thing. My father said that when he was in school, the bathrooms were still separated by color. When he told me this, my reaction was shock and disbelief. I was sitting on the back of his truck while he was telling me about the world he had lived in, and I couldn't imagine that kind of life. Now, looking back, I realize it wasn't that long ago that life was segregated that way, as scary as that sounds. I also realize that we are all currently living in a similar world. Racism is still very prevalent in America, even if some people don't like to admit it. As a nation, we need to educate people about racism and how it affects many different minorities.

I didn't grow up around African American people as a child; of course, there were some African American students in my school, but I never put myself out there with the black kids as I did with the white kids; I was afraid they wouldn't like me. Little did I know, racism was already taking effect on me at a young age. I lived in a nice neighborhood and was very fortunate to have the things I had. Something I remember when I was a child was my mom locking the car doors when she would see someone walking outside; that someone was almost always a black man. My mother would always talk about how black men and kids behaved badly, and most of the time would leave their families. As a child, I didn't see how color could predict someone's future, but since the information came from my mother's mouth, I assumed it was correct. However, something I didn't realize until I was a teenager was that my mother's point of view was part of a larger, systemic form of racism. Systemic racism is when society as a whole is racist. Even members of some minority groups become racist towards their own race. This is called internalized racism.

When I started doing research as I grew up, I discovered that I am privileged in America because I am white. I realized I'm not seen as a threat; I'm a white middle-class female. I wouldn't be pulled over and questioned for no reason by a police officer. There weren't hurtful stereotypes about me. White people need to recognize their privilege because the more we educate ourselves on others' struggles, the better chance we have at becoming a better society.

Recent events have shown that police officers and black communities have a lot of tension, and I personally think it has to do with officers being racist, even if they don't know they are. Too many black lives have been lost due to ignorant police officers. This past summer, a police shooting happened in Baton Rouge, Louisiana, resulting in the death of Alton Sterling. I never imagined something this horrific would happen where I live. It spiked extreme racial tension in Louisiana and was on the national news. Incidents similar to this that occurred in Ferguson, Missouri, and Baltimore seemed so far away. I soon realized I was very wrong, and that I shouldn't have seen those events as something foreign. Some officers racially profile blacks and see them as dangerous or a threat. How can a skin color be threatening? Regardless of what other people will argue, I believe if Alton Sterling had been white, he would still be alive today.

Something that stemmed from the police shooting was the term "All Lives Matter." People have been using that term to combat the Black Lives Matter movement. People who are using the "All Lives Matter" phrase are trying to silence the black community's expression of oppression. They are trying to silence blacks' voices because they don't identify with their struggles. Black Americans have had to experience oppression for hundreds of years. The United States needs to take a step back and look at itself. What black kids are witnessing now is what their grandparents protested to stop. It's like we went back to the sixties with the discrimination and the riots. We should learn from the past instead of repeating it. Isn't that why we learn about history in the first place?

NO MORE GETTING AWAY WITH IT

When I was in elementary school, in February we would have Black History Month programs. These programs taught me what African Americans went through while I was a young child and before I was born. During the programs, certain teachers would have students present biographical information or re-create speeches originally made by important historical figures. Some of the students would act as Rosa Parks, Martin Luther King Jr. or Frederick Douglass. The programs would be held during school hours in a room called the Blue Room. The Blue Room was a big room with blue walls and a big stage. While some teachers and students would be working on preparing the stage and presentations, others would decorate and make sure they had the correct background for certain parts of the play. The programs taught me a lot about the historical mistreatment of African Americans. They made me rethink the issue of racism. I thought it was dead and gone, but that simply isn't the case.

One night in July 2016, I was at home watching television and suddenly I received a text message from my friend. They sent a link and I clicked on it, not knowing what I was going to see. I saw a black man with a red shirt and jeans on and two white policemen. One policeman had blonde hair and the other one had black hair. The black man and the policemen were having an encounter with one another. I immediately knew something was going to happen because black men being killed by policemen had clearly been an issue over the previous months. I was unclear about what had led up to the confusion between the black man and the policemen, but as I continued watching the video, I asked myself why the cops were so aggressive. Did he say something wrong? The officers were screaming and hollering and had the man on the ground. Suddenly, I heard a gunshot. My heart and mouth dropped after I saw the man get shot. I started to tear up because all I could think about was his family. I instantly thought about my dad, brothers, and other male family members because it could have been one of them. The next day, I found out the man's name was Alton Sterling because the video was all over the news, and the incident had become the trending topic in Baton Rouge, Louisiana. Alton Sterling was the father of five children and was selling CDs outside of a store at the time the incident occurred.

On September 16, 2016, there was another incident: in Tulsa, Oklahoma. A forty-year-old black man named Terence Crutcher was shot by a white female police officer named Betty Shelby. Terence Crutcher had children and was enrolled in a community college. I was home scrolling through social media and saw a video of the man standing in the road because he was having trouble with his vehicle. According to police reports, two people called and stated that an abandoned vehicle was blocking the street and a man was running away; they warned that the vehicle was going to blow up. After the calls, Officer Shelby arrived at the scene. The officer later stated that Terence Crutcher wasn't cooperating with her instructions. As I watched the video, I saw that more police officers came to the scene, and as Terence was walking back to his vehicle, he had his hands up and was soon shot. He was unarmed; he had no weapons on him or in the vehicle. The most shocking thing to me that occurred in the video was when someone made the statement "He looks like a bad dude." He was another black male judged on the basis of his race. He did nothing wrong, and the entire situation could have been handled differently.

After I saw the videos of Alton Sterling and Terence Crutcher, I started to wonder what the world was coming to. Everything I learned from those black history programs started to come back into my head. I started asking myself, Is racism still real? Are we still in a world filled with hate? I started to question whether police were here to protect us or to kill African Americans. Citizens are supposed to go to police and look at police as people who can protect them. But how can we do that if we are black; when all we hear and see is them stereotyping black men?

Some police use their authority to take advantage of people. They feel that they have the right to judge and speak to others however they choose and to kill innocent people whenever they want. What about the families that suffer because they have lost a loved one? Some of the people that were killed have children, and those children will never get to see their loved ones again. Those children have to grow up and go through life without someone who meant the world to them. It's not fair for someone to lose a loved one over something that could have been solved another way. There are so many ways for police to solve issues, but for some reason shooting is too often the solution to the problem. How can that be fair?

IAN

HISTORY REPEATED IS
HISTORY CREATED

When we are young kids, we all have many fantasies and dreams of becoming someone who people look up to. Usually, kids want to become firefighters, professional athletes, doctors, nurses, and even police officers. Typically, these are people who are known to "save the day" or make big things happen that can always be remembered. As a young black man in America, I want to be someone who will be remembered. I believe every person wants to be remembered for something, especially those who are living for a purpose or for a cause.

Police officers are known to be our heroes, aren't they? I remember people at work talking about Alton Sterling being killed by police officers, and I was not aware of what had happened. I'm a very busy man, shifting between work, school, the gym, and time set aside for myself and my family. The job that I have consists of dealing with people all day long. I'm a customer service representative who answers calls and assists in meeting the needs of any and all customers I speak with. Something that stands out to me is how one can build a relationship with another person simply talking over the phone, and the key about that is that neither of us knows what the other looks like. It's not about skin color or stereotypes, but more about attitude, personality, and what I can do to help someone else. That is my full-time job, and with everything else filling my time, I never watch the news. To me, it's always reporting the same things: weather, sports and murders. I can check the weather on my phone, and I keep up with sports enough to know what is going on. I'm big into fitness, and many times I have been told, "You are what you eat." Well, I feel the same thing goes for the mind. Why fill your head up with negativity daily when it's something you don't want to hear? That is just time wasted.

But this news about the shooting of Alton Sterling was something I did want to hear. It was not the fact that it was a black male who had been killed by police officers. It was the fact that we as a nation should be past this type of police brutality. I was recently reading into black history after having a conversation with one of my coworkers about how the old times used to be for blacks. We are all familiar with how segregated this country used to be, going all the way down to having separate water fountains for each race to drink from. Great men and women such as Rosa Parks, Martin Luther King Jr., and Malcolm X each made a difference in the world, pushing forward for blacks to become equal under the law with everyone else. Isn't that word something? "Equals." Through trials and tribulations, this became a success for the black culture; sometimes things do change for the better and rearrange to still suit people's needs. Then why is this racial tension and police brutality still brewing?

I watched clips, read articles, and listened to people's opinions to gain a better perspective as to . . . why? At the end of every statement, it was always left as another black man being killed. Days go by, and every day you get on social media just to see another clip of some type of riot, protest, personal statement, blog or post about how we need to come together and better ourselves.

Black Panthers. Black Lives Matter. All Lives Matter. Blue Lives Matter. Black people vs. police. These topics were all being talked about and spread about. White people even began to argue that the Black Lives Matter movement was a group, considering it a new name or side group to the Black Panthers that was formed to fight against police. I never commented on anything anyone said or even tried to talk about it too much for that matter. I felt it was best to keep my mouth shut for the time being because one never knows who is listening and whether what a person is asking you is to be used for some purpose. The only thing I ever said was, "This is pure chaos, and eventually someone won't be able to take it anymore. Someone is going to snap and it will get worse."

July 7, 2016. Ex-Army veteran Micah Xavier Johnson took shots on law enforcement in Dallas, Texas, at what was to be a peaceful protest. Lo and behold, what I had predicted to a coworker was right. This was the start of a war among innocent police officers. Like they say, though, all it takes is one bad act to set off a chain of events. The man who first shot Alton Sterling had started the chain reaction. . . . Sitting there in my room watching an innocent civilian live capture this on Facebook put me in disbelief. Handguns, rifles, and explosives ring off, and the fear of that civilian was unheard of. During the next days, in the news all anyone talked about were Alton Sterling, Micah Johnson, police brutality, and deaths.

Driving through my city on the weekend to enjoy myself was no longer a normal activity. There are cops on every corner, police sirens flying through the air, and people chatting about what is going to happen next. Innocent people can't even enjoy themselves due to all the protesting and rioting going on. I feel that the protesting is a great way to make a statement, but only if it's done peacefully. That is why you're actually out there, not to just be seen in the crowd posting pictures on Facebook and Instagram to show you're a part of the movement. I feel like what a lot of people do not understand is that it's not about exposure, but about what you're exposing! I wanted no part of any protests because all I ever saw was a bunch of people rioting and getting in police officers faces. That was just plain stupid and ignorant, if you ask me. One might also ask, "Well, why don't you go out there and start your own protest?" To me, protesting can be done in more than one way, other than just going into the street and making a scene.

I remember on one Sunday of a great weekend, I was getting up to get ready to go to church. I was running late, though. The morning did not feel like a Sunday, as I heard the sound of sirens whizzing down my street and choppers flying over my house. I thought to myself, This sounds like the end of the world! I turned the TV on, and there it was once again. A man at Benny's gas station spraying down police officers! This gas station was no further than five minutes from my house. That explained all the sirens and chopper sounds. The first clip I saw was on Facebook of a man across the street from the shooting, and you could hear the sound of an automatic rifle being let loose. Once again, I could only imagine the innocent police officers being killed. This man was in broad daylight, just slaying police officers! I thought, God when will this all come to an end?

A new work week began the next day, and I couldn't fail to notice how all week the forecast called for rain, 80-100 percent every single day, including the weekend.

PART III

The Flood

JANEE'

THAT LITTLE GIRL'S VOICE

I remember the strong winds and our blue-black apartment complex after our neighborhood's surge protectors failed the night before. Mama and I were coming from the store to gather groceries and supplies for evacuation when we witnessed the menacing quietude in our empty neighborhood. Mama had lit a candle to illuminate each of the three bedrooms and the bathroom. The strong winds picked up through the night, so much that I heard them whistle. I remember being afraid and anticipating 6:45 a.m., when the light of day should come through my window. I had my own room, and that had to be one of the only times I wish I didn't. The sound of the tree branch on the rooftop of the apartment building reminded me of rats running through an attic. The combination of the whistling winds, the repetitious rhythm of the knocking tree, and the snoring of all five of my family members drove me insane! I knew I had to get some sleep; Mama planned to leave New Orleans at daybreak. I was excited about us taking a "road trip," but I had not the slightest idea why. However, I did overhear Mama and T.T. saying something about a Category 5.

On the way to Dallas, the nine of us were cramped into Mama's eight-passenger minivan. The baby for sure needed a car seat, which made things even more uncomfortable for the two of us who had to sit on either side of him. We often took rest stops and meal breaks on the way there. We kids ate our snacks in the van with the two sliding doors open and all the windows down while Daddy pumped the gas. Mama had to change and feed the baby before we began moving for another two hours. My brothers and two cousins played childish hand games in the backseat while I played Centipede on my first flip phone. When we arrived in Dallas, Mama woke us up to see the "Welcome to Dallas" sign. We pulled up to the hotel, and Daddy checked us in. The hotel on the first night was fairly nice. A bed for my parents and the baby, a bed for T.T. and my two cousins, and a pullout for my brothers and me. We slept comfortably after learning that nothing had yet happened to New Orleans. I didn't feel the severity of the situation until the next day.

The adults were up and looking at the news. My parents were hugging while Mama cried. I asked Mama, "What's wrong?" She never answered; she just hugged me. My dad said to the children, "Y'all pay attention; that's New Orleans." I remember looking at the television, seeing that red "LIVE" alert in the top left corner. I saw water covering houses up to the rooftops. I saw people waving and jumping for help on top of buildings. A man and his dog were floating in an empty refrigerator down a flooded street. The wind was too strong for the weatherman to stand in one place to narrate what was happening behind him. Something inside me was so sad to see that, yet I still didn't comprehend completely. "Call her again, baby!" Mama exclaimed. "Baby, the phone service in New Orleans is disconnected," Daddy said to her calmly. "I promise Mama is fine," he said confidently but unsure. I slowly caught on and began to feel knots in my belly. "Is Maw still in New Orleans?" I asked with tears streaming from my eyes. All of the adults looked around at each other with an uncanny expression.

"Maw will be fine, my baby," Mama said. Daddy opened the door quickly. "I guess we'll have to extend our stay," he said.

It was to everyone's surprise that the price of the hotel room had risen. Apparently, the check-in rates went through the roof throughout the night in expectation of arriving Hurricane Katrina evacuees. We ended up having to check into an inn by nightfall. It was all we could afford. We had to stretch our money over the course of that time; no one knew how long that would be. Mama and T.T. went to the store to gather some groceries while Daddy, the kids, and I stayed behind in the small room. When they came back, Mama stretched a long strip of connected paper towels across the bed to prepare ham sandwiches for everyone. We watched the news all night while the kids were sleeping side by side at the foot of the bed. Every news station displayed different scenes of the city's damage due to Hurricane Katrina. Suddenly, Mama's phone rang. It was Maw. Mama put her on speaker, and she let us all know that she was just fine. She couldn't call us until she had made it to an area with telephone service. Maw got in contact with a family member who lived in Baton Rouge so that she could have a place to sleep. I was thrilled that she was OK, but my mind wondered about where we were going to live now that our home was under water.

The next morning, we hit the road around 10:00 a.m. The drive to Baton Rouge was windy; the sky was gray, and the trees were dancing in the wind. It was a little scary for us, but we had to make the drive. One of our family members had invited us to stay in their two-bedroom apartment. Though we were comforted by our family members, there was still no place like home. After a week in Baton Rouge, I began to miss home. I missed going to school, having my own room, and playing outside with my friends. I called some of my friends from home, and all of their numbers were disconnected. I developed crazy thoughts in my head about them all drowning under water. I was terrified of the water in the bathtub, though I never told anyone. Mama told me to pray every night that our friends and family were all OK. Several weeks passed and I still hadn't heard from any of my friends. Some family members called, but still none of my friends. "You'll make some new friends at your new school," Mama said. "New friends? New school?" I cried. "I was just getting used to my *new school* in New Orleans."

We didn't come to Baton Rouge with much. Our wardrobe consisted of hand-me-downs from cousins and clothes that were donated by churches and community caregivers. I started my first day of middle school in Baton Rouge wearing a long khaki skirt that was a little too large around my waist, and a blue ruffled collar shirt. My hair was in a neatly brushed bun, and my glasses sat big and round on my nose. Mama thought I was adorable, but the kids at school called me the Virgin Mary . . . and my *favorite* nickname, Blackie N.O. Another girl from New Orleans they called Red Bone N.O., as if we didn't have names. There was something so significant about us being from New Orleans; nearly every day we would have people asking us to pronounce specific words because they enjoyed our accents. Yet they teased us about being on the rooftops of our homes and wearing our uniforms with Shaq's StarBury shoes instead of the latest Jordans. I was picked on about my puffy hair because all Mama could do with it was create simple styles; at the time, we lacked the materials needed to style my hair better. I remember one girl asked me for my FEMA number so that she could get back the money that New Orleans people were receiving from her Mama's taxes. Where would a child hear such a thing to repeat it?

It was clear to the people of New Orleans that by *some* people of Baton Rouge we were not wanted. I remember Mama having to walk me to the bus stop in the morning to ensure that the other children didn't pick on me; well, the picking began on the bus ride to school. "I bet y'all New Orleans people packed in that house like a bunch of Mexicans trying to run away from Katrina!" a boy shouted aloud from the back of the bus. Everyone laughed, including the bus driver. "Y'all asses need to go home, sucking up our air and drinking up our water!" said another boy sitting next to him. Clearly, those kids were ignorant, and clearly they had heard these things in conversations held between people other than their peers. I overheard two of my teachers saying how annoyed they were about having to add more kids to their roster. "They need to make a school where all these lil' New Orleans thugs and heathens can go!" one of them quietly exclaimed. "Hell, this is putting more work on us. We have to welcome them in, get them familiar, and catch them up on the shit that they missed. This is not our dilemma!"

Eleven years passed. The historic flood of Baton Rouge occurred weeks before my fall semester of college. Some people lost cars, some lost *stuff,* and some people lost their homes and had to rebuild. Suddenly, everyone understood the Hurricane Katrina struggle. While my heart goes out to everyone who lost their things and homes, I am a firm believer in reaping what you sow. The people of New Orleans felt rejection in a time of need. Not all people, but some adults and children made my experience so intolerable that I had to pretend to be hurt or sick to not attend school on some days. I cried often about being different from, yet so similar to, this neighboring group of individuals. Baton Rouge and New Orleans are only about seventy miles apart in distance, yet some of us evacuees felt so alienated. Some kids were being laughed at for wearing faded navy blue shirts and "high-water" pants to school because that was all they had. Gang fights consisted of segregated city groups fighting under the idea that one city was better than the other. We were addressed in unison: The New Orleans People versus Jigga City (Baton Rouge). Sad, isn't it? Well, why are some people's mouths poked out because they lost cars during the flood, which are not being replaced fast enough? Why are some people mad because there is no money saved for damages due to the fact that no one knew that catastrophe was approaching? Why was the very same guy who made fun of my off-brand shoes eleven years ago standing in line to receive a rescue/care box? Because he is a victim of the flood.

The sad truth is that at some time, everyone will need assistance. *Stuff* isn't so easily replaced, and great tolls can be taken on the lives of those who fall victim to mother nature, and in life, period. Both the flood of Baton Rouge and Hurricane Katrina taught me that the stuff we treasure can be easily taken away in an instant. Do not judge someone's life by the chapter you walked in on. My family and I struggled to see happy days after Hurricane Katrina. By the grace and love of God, we are resigned here in Baton Rouge in comfortable homes, and we are doing quite well for a couple of Katrina refugees. We should all extend a hand where we are needed. Welcome those who need a home, for you know not what they have been through. It is time for our community to wake up and quit acting as if they are exempt from struggle. There are innocent people being murdered in our community, and there are times of need that require more than just our condolences. We, the people, will be held accountable if we do nothing.

THE GREAT FLOOD OF 2016

We stood watching the local news channel. That was all that was covering it. We saw highways, businesses, and homes sitting in a brown lake of water. I turned on my phone and saw videos and pictures of schools and homes surrounded by water. My parents, my siblings, and I were all gathered around the TV. "This is the worst flood that's ever hit the U.S.," said my dad. In fact it was one of the worst in history. We were lucky. We were safe inside our home, with little flooding in our backyard. We knew that we needed to help others.

My sister came up with the idea to go and help at a shelter. She found out that there was a shelter in our town. "They need volunteers," she said. My parents were hesitant since all of the roads were flooded and because of the continuous rainfall, but we decided to go and help. It was a small shelter in our town civic center. There were few people affected in our town.

The next day we found out the house of my mom's aunt and uncle had been flooded beyond repair. They had to be evacuated to a shelter at a middle school in Central, Louisiana. We wanted to help them, so we planned out a safe route and drove to the school. When we got there, I was a bit surprised. The school was filled with victims. There were at least thirty people sitting along the front of the entrance, outside of the gymnasium. All they had were a few garbage bags of stuff they had saved and donations. There was a line of about forty people waiting for food in the parking lot. Inside the gymnasium, dozens of people were sitting in chairs and sleeping on cots or blankets. Kids were walking around, looking for something to do. There were dogs lying beside their owners. Even though they had nothing, people didn't complain. They were thankful when they were handed food. They respected each other's property and space. The people I talked to did not act like victims of a flood; they were happy to have shelter and food to eat. They had great morale.

Over the next few weeks, I saw the community come together to rebuild. The victims and those who were not affected began repairing the damage. There was work being done everywhere. As I was driving down Greenwell Springs Road to go to my church, I saw the damage. There were ditches filled with carpet, sheetrock, and furniture; stuff that people had lived with their entire lives was thrown in a pile. People were hard at work to get their lives back to normal.

When I got to my church, Greenwell Springs Baptist, there were big trailers in the parking lot. They belonged to Samaritan's Purse, a humanitarian aid organization. I walked around the church to see what was going on. There was a small crew making meals for victims and workers. I learned that there were teams of volunteers, from Samaritan's Purse and my church, out fixing damage to homes.

Over the next few days, I went by my church to help hand out food at the supply drive the church had set up. People would drive up with trailer loads of supplies to drop off. We collected so many cases of water that we had to start putting some outside.

The church youth building had been flooded, and there were at least a dozen kids from my youth group helping to repair it.

They were there every day until they could go back to school. I was pushing a dolly with bleach bottles on it when the youth pastor's assistant, Chandler, asked me to help him load his truck with clothes. "We have to bring this to another shelter because we don't have any more room," he said. So we loaded up and drove into town to drop off the supplies. People at the first shelter we went to said that it was already packed with clothes and couldn't take any more. I found it incredible that within a week, most of the area shelters had been overloaded with supplies. I began to understand what an amazing community I lived in. After two more stops, we finally found a place that would take our supplies. The amusing thing was, the place where they kept their supplies was filled up, literally. They had a semi out back where they were putting excess supplies. It was almost halfway full!

The people of Louisiana did not hesitate to lend a hand. However, the people who lived here were not the only ones who helped out. People drove here from all over the country to cook food and donate supplies. I remember one particular group, a basketball team of at least ten high-schoolers, that drove all the way from Atlanta, Georgia, to help out. The country was beginning to hear of the crisis in Louisiana.

After a few weeks passed, the national media finally began reporting on the flood in southern Louisiana. Donald Trump visited my church to donate supplies and relief funds. Political views aside, I appreciated him helping out my community. The first report I saw on national media was Sean Hannity from Fox News. He gave an hour-long report of the flood and interviewed many people from my church. The world finally knew.

Through personal experience, I was able to see the incredible spirit of community in southern Louisiana. People did not hesitate to help victims. Victims did not hesitate to thank them in return. They were able to rise above their situation. Both victims and those unaffected showed great character.

J. J. ANGEL

STILL WATER RUNS DEEP

E ver since I was a child, I've had dreams that were larger than my hands could contain, and yet my mind always found a way to capture my imagination of the world. I was gifted with extraordinary superhuman abilities, and when someone was in trouble, I was always there to save the day. I was a superhero of intellect in a dystopian world divided by the far reaches of light and deep depths of darkness: the Elites and the Retreats of society. I was unstoppable. I was unshakable. I was an uninhibited force to be reckoned with.

In reality, I was an introverted oddball, a low spirit with a fragile heart, a short kid with an even shorter attention span. If you barked I would cower, and if you came forth I would flee. If you talked down to me, I would surely believe your words to be true. For how could I contend with the reality of my own ignorance when I was not self-aware? As the years progressed, my dreams of being that inspiration, that spark of light, uttering those words of wisdom that merited a standing ovation, were washed away.

One night in my dreams, it was almost as if I could hear the hands of one thousand Elites coming together after I had given a glorious testimony. I noticed that the sounds of their applause were accompanied by periods of distant rumbling. Was this what it sounded like to have a heart beating with ambition? When I opened my eyes from my slumber, I was covered in a blanket of darkness. I wasn't a stranger to the night nor the wee hours of the morning. This was normally the time I would get up and prepare for work, and even though I was off that day, my mind reassured me that there was something I needed to do, and so I waited. Sometimes repetition has a way of guiding humanity.

The date was August 13, 2016, and the time was around four in the morning. The sounds from outside continued to pour into my ears, and when I lifted myself up, I realized the applause of the Elites were the heavy rains still battering up against my rooftop. "So it's still raining," I mumbled. A flash of lightning spilled through the breaks of the window blinds, illuminating the interior of my living room for a few seconds. It wasn't long before a deep rumbling sound echoed over my home, causing me to flinch. Well, there goes my ambition. My eyes tightened and my skin began to crawl as the thunder mixed with sounds of falling rain to create a foreboding melody. Something didn't sit right within my spirit at that moment. It had been raining for nearly two days straight, and there had been no signs of it slackening anytime soon. I made my way over to the window, parting a section of the blinds into a horizontal slit. I couldn't see what was going on outside at that moment, but a swift jolt of lightning enlightened me. My eyes bucked for a split second and my heart jumped back before my mind could even process what I had witnessed. There was a stream of water drifting across the midpoint of the gate in front of my home. I quickly closed the blinds, cutting my line of vision abruptly.

"What in the heck?" I mumbled.

My eyes must have been deceiving me. The blanket of darkness was placing a veil over my face because there was no way the water had risen that high. After these drifting thoughts, I decided to flip a switch controlling a light outside. I peered through the blinds once again. The water was still there. The sound of heavy rain continued to flood my ears as the outside porch light illuminated the wavering currents streaming their way through the fence. Even after seeing all of this, my eyes still didn't want to believe what my mind and heart already knew. I walked out the front door onto the porch of my slightly elevated structure and saw water everywhere. I couldn't see the grass in my front yard. There was no sign of the sidewalk leading to the front gate, and the heavy raindrops were dancing on ripples that echoed over what was once a visible street.

It was like my home was sailing over the desolate waves of darkness and I was the man lost at sea. I glanced down and saw the water steadily approaching the highest step of my porch, and I backed into my home and closed the front door. The area where I lived was also a location where a number of senior citizens resided, so I decided to call a neighbor and check on them.

"Hey, are you OK?" I asked.

"I'm fine. Where are you?" she asked.

"I'm still at home," I replied.

"Oh, you need to get out of there now, then!" she said.

I could hear the sound of several low voices filling up the background through my smartphone.

"Where are you?" I asked, squinting my eyes.

She took a light breath. "The fire department came by last night and evacuated everyone to a shelter," she said.

Silence kissed my lips for a few seconds.

"Wait, what? I must have slept through that somehow," I replied.

After our brief conversation had ended, I called the authorities and notified them of my location. I was told that someone would be out to rescue me when they could. After I got off of my smartphone, I stepped back outside and realized that I was indeed stuck until help arrived. I went back in and paced from one room into the next, waiting and wondering what I should do. My thoughts were drowning in confusion and disbelief. I'd never been in a situation like this. I'm from northern Louisiana, and I'd never seen water this high near my house. What should I do? Did I need to start gathering things? What should I grab first? Maybe I should make my way towards the roof?

I paced from my living room into my bedroom and back every few seconds. The seconds then turned into minutes until an hour had passed. I walked over towards the window again. Still no sign of anyone. Should I even be surprised? The water was as far as I could see, and so was the chaos probably. I'm sure the rescue situation was dire in my area. I slowly opened my front door and walked out onto my porch and looked at the murky water continuing to rise steadily. I paced back and forth, wondering what I should do. I was far away from any family, and there was still no sign of help. I decided that I should take a chance through the waters to get to higher ground. My mind began forecasting the several possible outcomes from me stepping down into an unknown murky abyss. My legs began to quiver while my thoughts continued to overflow. I was beginning to second-guess myself, but it was either now or never.

The sensation of blood flowing through my veins and merging into my heart woke my senses. I could taste wet adrenaline on the tip of my tongue, and my eyes were dead set on the front gate just up ahead. I needed to get to higher ground, and to do that I had to go through the water. I quickly backtracked inside my home and grabbed a spare shirt, a pair of work pants, my Chromebook, and a few other personal items, and placed them in a small backpack before I stepped outside onto the porch again. I walked up towards the edge and said a prayer. I began to make my way down each step into the water, finally reaching the lowest point my feet could touch. A channel of lukewarm water shot up my legs, eventually wrapping around my thighs, violating my privacy. The amount of discomfort was beyond belief. I couldn't see through the water, but saw everything displaced onto its surface. There were muddy sticks and grass, fleeing insects, frogs, and dirty trash floating all over. I took a deep breath and slowly made my way over towards my fence and walked out into the flooded street.

It took me about twenty minutes to cautiously stride through the murky abyss until I could see a section of the street emerging from the watery depths up ahead. It was leading towards a main road, and I was almost there. I glanced out of the corner of my eye and saw a row of bubbles hit the surface several feet away from where I was wading. The bubbles surfaced twice, just seconds apart. What is that? An animal maybe? I turned my head and kept wading until I finally stepped onto a side street with tiny pockets of water dripping from the cuff of my blue jeans. When I made my way onto the main road, the sounds of lamenting sirens filled my eardrums. I turned towards my left and, looking farther down, could see the police station surrounded by a pool of water. There was a firetruck in the middle of the road along with several other police vehicles scattered about. So the flood got to them too, it seemed. I glanced at a towering street sign just a few feet away from my position. The road was named Highland. How co-incidental it was for me to see such a thing at that moment. I had just waded through what probably was the dirtiest water ever, and I still managed to have a drop of humor tucked under a dry sleeve. I turned away and looked back down the other end of Highland Road, which wasn't flooded. I took a deep breath and walked to work as I would have on any other regular day in the past.

When I got to the news station, I didn't say anything about what had happened to me, though my soggy jeans and shoes surely re-layed the tale. It was then that I learned of the true devastation caused by the heavy rains. This was an unprecedented event that affected thousands of people all around Baton Rouge and its sister communities. No one was spared. Every gender, every sexuality, every ethnicity, and every race were now all under the same um-brella. The Historic Flood of 2016 had washed over us all.

FAMILY VS. FLOOD

I t was early in the morning of August 12, 2016, when we learned that our hometown, Albany, Louisiana, from which we had moved just a few months earlier, was under five to six feet of water. Altogether there were about five days of rain with a few short hour breaks. I didn't realize just how serious the rainfall had gotten until my cousin Dylan and my very best friend, Kellee, were forced to evacuate their homes. They only had a few minutes to gather personal belongings and load them into an eight-foot-tall army truck, which they depended on to carry them to safety. I remember how anxious I was to hear from them. I just wanted to hear their voices or get a "We made it, we're safe" text. Sadly, that text didn't come as the minutes turned into hours. My cousin Dylan was a real trouper that day. He assisted the elderly in his subdivision and carried them out on his back to the tall truck to be taken to safety. You can probably imagine how relieved I was to be informed a few hours later that Dylan and Kellee were just fine. All seemed to be well at this point until we learned that the fire department was taking water, and so Dylan and his family had to leave the place they thought was their safe haven once more. Luckily, an old friend of my Pawpaw's brought them as far down my grandparents' road as he could, and that's where my Pawpaw and Uncle waited to bring them to that sand-colored house we all knew so well, which they thought would be their final stop. Surely, they thought, they could ride out the rest of the storm there.

Dylan and I have been the best of friends since we were in diapers. His dad and my mom are two of the youngest of seven children and just so happen to be twins. Dylan always looked out for me, sometimes a little too much. So imagine my concern when I got an alarming phone call from him later that day. Dylan is a tough, strong guy. He doesn't cry often, but when he's really upset he usually calls me. I can tell when something is wrong with him. The panic in his voice was overwhelming. I could hear the concern and quivering of his voice, which as always broke my heart. I will never forget his next few words as long as I live, and I'm sure neither will he. "It's coming in, Payge! It wasn't a few minutes ago; it was fine, and now it's not! It's flowing in—I don't know what to do. Pawpaw is trying to lift things up. . . ." Shortly after that, his mom took his phone and assured me everything was going to be all right, which was nice but didn't exactly ease my concern. The house I knew and loved so much as a child was now consumed by water. My Pawpaw is a strong man who worked hard for everything he had. He's strong on the outside, but somewhat soft on the inside. I can imagine he was concerned for my Mawmaw and the rest of the family before himself and frantically trying to do what he thought would help. As I thought about my family and their situation, I closed my eyes and tears streamed down my face. This was real life, this was happening. What could I do to help?

After I received that call from Dylan, my parents seemed alarmed. I guess they could see the concern and shock in my expression and immediately asked what had happened. Once I explained, my mom and I were on the phone with anyone and everyone we knew trying to send out a rescue team from town to help my family. After about an hour of nonstop phone calls to our friends nearby, there was still no hope. Luckily, my family members had made it out of my grandparents' home safely, but they were trapped with nowhere to go. My dad and Mr. Dub tried to go as far to them by truck as they could, but the water stopped them eventually. The roads started to disappear into large dark streams of water that only began to rise higher and higher. My family was surrounded by water in all directions, and the only hope for them was to take refuge at my Aunt Gracie's house at the end of their road and frantically wait for a call from us to see if we had found anyone to come rescue them.

It was then that we prayed. My whole family was now aware of the situation, and every one of us was praying. My family consists of roughly sixty people—and that's just immediate family. You can imagine how many prayer warriors we had on our side that night. What we didn't know was how soon our prayers would be answered. Night was approaching fast, and the rain still hadn't slackened. A few more hours of rain and Aunt Gracie's house would've started taking water, too. When there seemed to be no hope and we were running out of options, we learned that my aunt Carla had her own rescue plan in mind.

My Aunt Carla is fairly tall, has short brown hair, and is a little on the spunky side. She lived not too far from my grandparents and was determined to get them safely to her house, where they were high and dry. She wasn't 100 percent sure how well her plan would work, but she and her husband loaded up their aluminum flatboat and she drove. She drove as far towards my family as she could before she had to switch her means of transportation from truck to boat. By this time, night had fallen and the sky was pitch black. My grandparents, my Aunt Amy, Devyn, Dylan, and my Uncle Kurt were forced to wade through knee-deep water, which quickly became waste-deep water, to meet my Aunt Carla in her boat. Dylan told me later, "It was one of the craziest and scariest things I've ever done!" Anxiously, my parents, my younger sister, and I were waiting by our phones to hear that they had made it all right. That wait felt like a lifetime. It took about two and half hours for them to travel by boat and truck back to my Aunt Carla's house. They were safe. They made it. They were all right. That was the best news I had ever received! Everything was going to be fine, and they were going to be safe and sound. They ate, showered, and tried to rest as comfortably as could be expected. After taking refuge at four different places in one day, all of which were now consumed by water—for my cousins and my aunt; my grandparents had lost their home and most of their belongings—they had finally been awarded their safe haven. The safe haven they deserved!

A few weeks later, as our families and our town had begun to recover, my mom invited my family over to our house for what my grandparents thought was a surprise party for my dad's birthday. Actually, it was a big family dinner so that we could all be together and surprise them. They had lost all their pictures in their home, or so they thought. What they didn't know was that my cousin Mallory had their one and only wedding picture saved on a flash drive from their fiftieth wedding anniversary party, and she had it printed out and framed specially for them. So now they couldn't say they had no pictures for their new house. As Mallory explained to my grandparents and the rest of my family how she had the picture printed, the whole room was moved to tears. We have such a big and loving family. It is somewhat like the branches of a tree; we all grow in different directions, but our roots remain as one. And our roots are my grandparents; without them, this big family wouldn't exist. They've done so much for all of us, so now it is our turn to try and repay them. Although their home was unsalvageable and they are now trying to rebuild, what was not lost and will remain is their love, trust, and faith in God.

The walls of their home now carry the stench of mold. The buckling floors are starting to come up piece by piece. The pictures are soaked completely by the four feet of water that once flooded their home. Their clothes are soiled as well as all of their food. All the years' worth of hard work my Pawpaw had put into building that home was all washed away with one giant natural disaster, the flood of 2016. Their days are now spent salvaging what little they can and starting completely over again . . . this time five feet off the ground. In the few months that have passed since the flood, my Pawpaw and some family members have managed to frame my grandparents' new home almost completely. With a little blood, sweat, and tears, they'll continue working to build this home from the ground up. The flood may have taken the material items of people all over south Louisiana and left them homeless, forced to start over, but it didn't take one irreplaceable thing from us: our families.

TARA

THE NEW GIRL

When I was eight years old, I was in Mrs. Kerner's second grade class at Mandeville Elementary School. My mom and my teacher had many meetings about me being a "social butterfly." Basically, I couldn't stop talking and trying to be everyone's friend. One day at lunch, I remember seeing this little girl who was new. Of course, my first instinct was to go talk to her. I sat next to her with my lunch tray, and I introduced myself and asked if she liked her new school. The only response I got from her was "My parents say bad things about people like you." When she said that, I didn't understand what she meant, so I kept trying. I asked her question after question and told her about myself. Then, finally, she got up and walked away and didn't say a word. Of course, my feelings were hurt. I was eight years old and used to people talking to me and loving the attention I would give them.

When I got home that night, I talked to my mom about what happened, and she asked, "Was there anything different about the little girl that you noticed?" I just kept saying, "No. She was a girl like me." I was getting frustrated with my mom because she just kept asking me all of these weird questions. Then, finally, she just flat out asked me about the little girl's skin color, and I just said with an attitude, "She was darker than me, but that's not it, Mom." That was when she said, "Not everyone will get along, and everyone has their own reasons."

I didn't quite understood what she meant by that until I was older. I'm twenty-one years old now, and what my mom said that night when I was in second grade has stuck with me; it applies to some things that have happened recently in Baton Rouge. In the summer of 2016, a terrible tragedy happened to a man named Alton Sterling. It has impacted everyone in the local area. It has impacted people emotionally and affected everyone's sense of safety.

I was terrified when I saw the video of the shooting all over social media. I was just about to move to Baton Rouge for school; my best friend and I had everything planned. Then, when the shooting of Alton Sterling happened and protests erupted, my mom insisted that I not move to the area. I wasn't even allowed to go to Baton Rouge to visit my friends. Then the protests started getting out of hand, with nightly confrontations with police and people being hauled off to jail. Not long afterward, cops were killed in Dallas and in Baton Rouge, but revenge never solves anything. After everything that had already happened, all I could think about were the families who lost loved ones. My heart was broken for them.

Everyone thought Louisiana was doomed, that we would tear ourselves apart. Then the Great Flood of 2016 happened, and it was another tragic event. However, instead of just quitting and letting all of these terrible things destroy us, something ironic happened. The flood brought all of us together. It had complete strangers—of all races, might I add—pulling people to safety. Skin color didn't matter. This just proves that no matter what difficulties we face, we can come together as a whole and come out of it stronger than ever. Now, I'm not naive, and I know healing takes time and not all wounds are healed. We are human. We make mistakes, but we also have the power to make things better.

ACKNOWLEDGMENTS

Clarence Nero—Our leader, mentor and advisor. Thank you for your unwavering faith in our voices. Thank you for going above and beyond duties to show us the importance of courage. Through your eyes, you've created a vision that will stand as a landmark in history. Your belief in us was overwhelming.

The Other Editors—Carrie Causey, Shelisa Theus, and Eric Elliott, we are so grateful to all of you for believing in our work and taking time out of your busy schedules to edit our manuscript during final exam week. We know that was not an easy task.

Phil Smith *(Vice Chancellor of Economic Development)*—You have been an inspirational leader to us all. Thank you for opening up your door to us. We were in awe of your willingness to be support-ive of our voices. The effort you put into assisting us will not go unnoticed.

Gerri Hobdy—Although we did not work with you directly, we heard from Mr. Nero how much time and effort you put into making sure everything went as planned. Your support is greatly appreciated.

Dr. Gail Suberbielle and Dr. Sarah Barlow—As the dean and chairwoman, respectively, of Liberal Arts, we appreciate the fact that both of you encouraged and supported the editors and professors from the beginning and allowed our book to be used as a supplemental text inside English classes within your department. We are in awe of your belief in us.

Baton Rouge Participating Professors—The hours we spent covering papers with words from within, you all matched with your assistance in editing our narratives. We thank you for the countless hours spent making sure our voices were heard in the best way.

Stuart Bache—The vision you saw with us says it all. From the moment we shared our ideas, you showed passion for our cause. We thank you so much for bringing our vision to life and creating such a unique book cover. To know that you do book covers for authors like Stephen King is simply phenomenal and we are honored to have your work on the front of our book.

Sharika Mahdi—It was pleasure meeting you at Professor Nero's birthday party and agreeing to do the interior layout. We are so happy to work with you on this project!

Donna Perreault—We have not worked with you directly, but Mr. Nero showed us the notes you made on our stories. We couldn't have had a more talented and dedicated copy editor and we appreciate you so much.

Kevin McQuarn—Thank you for capturing our voices on video. Your dedication to our cause is appreciated.

Janet Hill—Professor Nero informed us that you were the featured editor on the amazing book *Freedom Writers* and that you were advising him on our book as well. We are beyond honored to know that your eyes and hands played a role in shaping our book. From the bottom of our hearts, thank you.

Voices from the Bayou would like to extend our greatest gratitude to the Baton Rouge Community College Foundation and The Bayou Soul Literary Conference. Thank you for supporting us.

The Baton Rouge Community College Foundation, Inc. (BRCC Foundation) is a non-profit corporation organized April 16, 1998, existing and operating for the purpose of securing recurring philanthropic support to advance, promote, and otherwise benefit the mission of Baton Rouge Community College, its faculty, and its students. The vision is to exemplify the highest standards of integrity, accountability, and transparency. The Foundation solicits private, voluntary contributions to advance and support the programs and facilities of BRCC; manages investments; and serves as steward for funds and other contributed assets.

Made in the USA
Columbia, SC
15 February 2019